1 9 8 7

AMPLITUDE

New and Selected Poems

OTHER BOOKS BY TESS GALLAGHER

Poetry

INSTRUCTIONS TO THE DOUBLE
UNDER STARS
WILLINGLY

Essays

A CONCERT OF TENSES

Short Stories

THE LOVER OF HORSES

Screenplay

DOSTOEVSKY (with Raymond Carver)

Tess Gallagher

AMPLITUDE

New and Selected Poems

GRAYWOLF PRESS / SAINT PAUL

Grateful acknowledgment is made to the editors and publishers of the following periodicals, in which the new poems in this collection were first published: *American Poetry Review*: "Message from the Sinecurist," "Their Heads Bent Toward Each Other Like Flowers," "The Story of a Citizen"; *Antaeus*: "His Shining Helmet; Its Horsehair Crest," "With Stars"; *Caliban*: "The Hands of the Blindman"; *Ironwood*: "Portrait of a Lighthouse Through Fog," "Simple Sonatina," "Bonfire"; *Milkweed Chronicle*: "Amplitude," "Sugar," "If Blood Were Not as Powerful as It Is"; *The New Yorker*: "The Borrowed Ones"; *The Paris Review*: "All Day the Light Is Clear"; *Parnassus*: "Present"; *Poetry*: "If Poetry Were Not a Morality," "Redwing," "Dim House, Bright Face," "Rijl," "Small Garden Near a Field"; *Seattle Review*: "In Maceio"; *Vogue*: "That Kind of Thing"; *ZYZZYVA*: "Cougar Meat."

The author offers her special thanks to Harold Schweizer and to Scott Walker for their help in the preparation of this collection.

Publication of this volume is made possible in part by a grant from the National Endowment for the Arts, and by contributions to Graywolf Press from many generous individuals, foundations and corporations. Graywolf is a member agency of United Arts.

Third printing

ISBN 1-55597-110-5
Library of Congress Catalog Card Number 87-81375

Published by GRAYWOLF PRESS
2402 University Avenue
Suite 203
Saint Paul, Minnesota 55114

Contents

I

from INSTRUCTIONS TO THE DOUBLE

II

from UNDER STARS

III

from WILLINGLY

IV

NEW POEMS

RAYMOND CARVER

"Words lead to deeds. . . . They prepare the soul, make it ready, and move it to tenderness."

SAINT TERESA

I

from

INSTRUCTIONS

TO THE DOUBLE

Kidnaper

He motions me over with a question.
He is lost. I believe him. It seems
he calls my name. I move
closer. He says it again, the name
of someone he loves. I step back pretending

not to hear. I suspect
the street he wants
does not exist, but I am glad to point
away from myself. While he turns
I slip off my wristwatch, already laying a trail
for those who must find me
tumbled like an abandoned car
into the ravine. I lie

without breath for days among ferns.
Pine needles drift
onto my face and breasts
like the tiny hands
of watches. Cars pass.
I imagine it's him
coming back. My death
is not needed. The sun climbs again
for everyone. He lifts me
like a bride

and the leaves fall from my shoulders
in twenty-dollar bills.
"You must have been cold," he says
covering me with his handkerchief.
"You must have given me up."

Instructions to the Double

So now it's your turn,
little mother of silences, little
father of half-belief. Take up
this face, these daily rounds
with a cabbage under each arm
convincing the multitudes
that a well-made-anything
could save them. Take up
most of all, these hands
trained to an ornate piano
in a house on the other side
of the country.

I'm staying here
without music, without
applause. I'm not going
to wait up for you. Take
your time. Take mine
too. Get into some trouble
I'll have to account for. Walk
into some bars alone
with a slit in your skirt. Let
the men follow you on the street
with their clumsy propositions, their
loud hatreds of this and that. Keep
walking. Keep your head
up. They are calling to you – slut, mother,
virgin, whore, daughter, adultress, lover,
mistress, bitch, wife, cunt, harlot,
betrothed, Jezebel, Messalina, Diana,

Bathsheba, Rebecca, Lucretia, Mary,
Magdelena, Ruth, you – Niobe,
woman of the tombs.

Don't stop for anything, not
a caress or a promise. Go
to the temple of the poets, not
the one like a run-down country club,
but the one on fire
with so much it wants
to be done with. Say all the last words
and the first: hello, goodbye, yes,
I, no, please, always, never.

If anyone from the country club
asks if you write poems, say
your name is Lizzie Borden.
Show him your axe, the one
they gave you with a silver
blade, your name engraved there
like a whisper of their own.

If anyone calls you a witch,
burn for him; if anyone calls you
less or more than you are
let him burn for you.

It's a dangerous mission. You
could die out there. You
could live forever.

Breasts

The day you came
this world got its hold on me.
Summer grass and the four of us pounding hell
out of each other for god knows what
green murder of the skull.
Swart nubbins, I noticed you then,
my mother shaking a gritty rag from the porch
to get my shirt on this minute. Brothers,
that was the parting of our ways, for then
you got me down by something else than flesh.
By the loose skin of a cotton shirt
you kept me to the ground
until the bloody gout hung in my face like a web.

Little mothers, I can't find your children.
I have looked in a man
who moved through the air like a god.
He brought me clouds
and the loose stars of his goings.
Another kissed me on a pier in Georgia
but there was blood on his hands,
bad whiskey in the wind. The last one,
he made me a liar until I stole
what I could not win. Loves,
what is this mirror you have left me in?

I could have told you at the start
there would be trouble
from other hands, how the sharp mouths
would find you where you slept.

But I have hurt you as certainly
with cold sorrowings as anyone,
have come the long way
over broken ground to this softness.
Good clowns, how could I know, all along
it was your blundering mercies kept me alive
when heaven was a luckless dream.

The Woman Who Raised Goats

Dear ones, in those days it was otherwise.
I was suited more to an obedience
of windows. If anyone had asked,
I would have said: "Windows are my prologue."

My father worked on the docks
in a cold little harbor, unhappily
dedicated to what was needed
by the next and further
harbors. My brothers
succeeded him in this, but when I,
in that town's forsaken luster, offered myself,
the old men in the hiring hall creeled
back in their chairs, fanning themselves
with their cards, with their gloves.
"Saucy," they said. "She's saucy!"

Denial, O my Senators,
takes a random shape. The matter
drove me to wearing
a fedora. Soon, the gowns, the amiable
forgeries: a powdery sailor, the blue silk
pillow given by a great aunt, my name
embroidered on it like a ship, the stitched
horse too, with its red plume and its bird eyes
glowing, glowing. There was the education
of my "sensibilities."

All this is nothing to you.
You have eaten my only dress, and the town
drifts every day now
toward the harbor. But always,
above the town, above
the harbor, there is the town,
the harbor, the caves and hollows
when the cargo of lights
is gone.

Beginning to Say No

is not to offer so much as a fist, is
to walk away firmly, as though
you had settled something foolish,
is to wear a tarantula in your buttonhole
yet smile invitingly, unmindful
how your own blood grows toward the irreversible
bite. No, I will not

go with you. No, that is not
alright. I'm not your sweet-dish, your
home-cooking, good-looking daf-
fodil. Yes is no
reason to slay the cyclops. No
will not save it. And the cricket, "Yes, yes."

Fresh bait, fresh bait!
The search for the right hesitation
includes finally
unobstructed waters. Goodbye,
old happy-go-anyhow, old shoe
for any weather. Whose
candelabra are you? Whose
soft-guy, nevermind, nothing-to-lose ant hill?

"And," the despised connective,
is really an engine
until it is *yes* all day, until a light
is thrown against a wall
with some result. And
there is less doubt, yes or no,
for whatever you have been compelled to say
more than once.

Coming Home

As usual, I was desperate.
I went through your house as if I owned it.
I said, "I need This, This and This."
But contrary to all I know of you,
you did not answer, only looked after me.

I've never seen the house so empty, Mother.
Even the rugs felt it, how little
they covered. And what have you done
with the plants? How thankfully
we thought their green replaced us.

You were keeping something like a light.
I had seen it before, a place you'd never been
or never came back from. It was a special way
your eyes looked out over the water. Whitecaps
lifted the bay and you said, "He should be here
by now."

How he always came back; the drinking,
the fishing into the night, all
the ruthless ships he unloaded.
That was the miracle of our lives. Even now
he won't stay out of what I have
to say to you.

But they worry me, those boxes
of clothes I left in your basement. Sometimes
I think of home as a storehouse, the more

we leave behind, the less
you say. The last time
I couldn't take anything.

So I'm always coming back like tonight,
in a temper, brushing the azaleas
on the doorstep. What did you mean
by it, this tenderness
that is a whip, a longing?

Black Money

His lungs heaving all day in a sulphur mist,
then dusk, the lunch pail torn from him
before he reaches the house, his children
a cloud of swallows about him.
At the stove in the tumbled rooms, the wife,
her back the wall he fights most, and she
with no weapon but silence
and to keep him from the bed.

In their sleep the mill hums and turns
at the edge of water. Blue smoke
swells the night and they drift
from the graves they have made for each other,
float out from the open-mouthed sleep
of their children, past banks and businesses,
the used car lots, liquor store, the swings in the park.

The mill burns on, now a burst of cinders,
now whistles screaming down the bay, saws jagged
in half light. Then like a whip
the sun across the bed, windows high with mountains
and the sleepers fallen to pillows
as gulls fall, tilting
against their shadows on the log booms.
Again the trucks shudder the wood-framed houses
passing to the mill. My father
snorts, splashes in the bathroom,

throws open our doors to cowboy music
on the radio. Hearts are cheating,
somebody is alone, there's blood in Tulsa.
Out the back yard the night-shift men rattle
the gravel in the alley going home.
My father fits goggles to his head.

From his pocket he takes anything metal,
the pearl-handled jack knife, a ring of keys,
and for us, black money shoveled
from the sulphur pyramids heaped in the distance
like yellow gold. Coffee bottle tucked in his armpit
he swaggers past the chicken coop,
a pack of cards at his breast.
In a fan of light beyond him
the *Kino Maru* pulls out for Seattle,
some black star climbing
the deep globe of his eye.

Clearing

The limbs are caught in each other
outside my window where the men
have entered the tree. Dead limbs
pile up on the shadows.
Now a saw goes up on a rope
and the ground man steps back
for what falls. I tell him my father
rigged spar trees in the west.
I need a reason to watch
this tree come down.

He uses his weight on the rope
like a saw, then backs off.
The chainsaw snarls and jaws.
Over him, the tree and the wind: sawdust
over my house.

If a tree goes down among others
it makes its whole length felt
as something lost and final, not
this slow dispossession
of parts. I have heard a whole tree cry out
in the clearings my father made.
But this tree snaps and shudders
and calms itself back
into silence.

From the street, the houses

seem to have stepped away.

In my window the likeness
of the tree goes on, the light
opening and gathering
over my desk, over what I cannot heal.

Even Now You Are Leaving

Not to let ourselves know
by a hand held too long, as this last,
words no part of any other, like a mule
trained to carry anything
and not mean it. Just so these lips
puffed from where you ran into yourself
in a car the night before, the wheel
turning through your mouth
like something you might have said.

I can't believe your face, that
it could fall from here, let alone
my own. Yet you prove it, the chin
large now as a forehead. Some nearness
has done this to you, or the lack
of it. That scheme you had
for making us rich, I want to tell you
it worked, though Alaska
stayed due north
and you never touched.

The spar tree axe
swings from a tree you rigged
to hold that clearing. I can't look up.
The tree's too white
and cedar an easy fire. Father,
some neglect is killing us all, but yours
has a name of its own: family,
something gone on without you, your eyes
ruined and terrible in a face
even now you are leaving.

The Coats

for Mary Kepler (1884–1966)

They made you complicated,
a new one each year
and underneath, the same
old print dress. Outside
under the maples you were smart
and garrulous on my grandfather's arm
walking down Valley Street
to the shops, talking into his silence
as into some idea of yourself
grown to your side.

Yet you loved telling how
you were engaged to another
the night he took you off
in his buckboard. Marriage too
came like an impulse
to turn against yourself. Life
caught you up in its clumsy arms
and danced you out of your Oklahoma
youth into the milltown
of my birth, you in your new coat,
leading me into the dimestore
to buy silk ribbons.

Shut in the closet, your coats
were a family of witnesses
who could not remember you.
They were waiting for the one
to send them all again
into the weather. Standing
before your mirror once

in the dark of the bedroom
I put myself into a heavy tweed
with its cold silk lining. The wide arms
were a hiding place; the hem
brushed my patent leather shoes.
It was a bargaining
that I should turn into the room,
your age about me like a sack.

I wanted to throw something over you
the day they carried you off
like a trophy in your silk lining.
Rosy and familiar you received each of us
in a housedress that denied you
were going anywhere. That year
the winter came over the ground
like a rich white pelt.
I thought of you accepting it,
something chosen, a comfort
that had sought you out
in the cold of the land.

The Horse in the Drugstore

wants to be admired.
He no longer thinks of what he has given up
to stand here, the milk-white reason
of chickens over his head in the night, the grass
spilling on through the day. No, it is enough
to stand so with his polished chest among the nipples
and bibs, the cotton, and multiple sprays, with his black lips
parted just slightly and the forehooves doubled back
in the lavender air. He has learned when maligned to snort
dimes and to carry the inscrutable bruise like a bride.

Cows, a Vision

for Porter Morris

Some monster bird, the barn
flings its shadow across the field
to the walnut grove. The cows
with milk-worn bodies muffle
its cry, the cry of riverbeds
gone white. In the rafters
the wings of swallows breathe
over eggs like eyes. If the sun
falls on them they must open
and fly. I was born that way,
some beak of light lifting a straw.

The cows were never born. They came
with the land, with the bucket
hanging in the well, with the iron
bed and the empty cat who slept
by the clock and ticked only
to your hand. You took it all
because it was the cat's dream
or the clock's or the empty bed
waiting. You filled everything,
the barn, the bucket, the bed,
even the empty dream and then
you built yourself a front porch
where, of an evening, you could
sit down to bullfrogs and rusty owls.

It was up to the cows after that
to keep things going. Their mouths
were always faithful, turning
like windmills the heavy heart

of the moon. For a moment toward dawn
or dusk the cows pause in their work
and a secret moon swells in them,
threatens to carry them over the barn
and away. When we die, I tell you,
that moon will find its stars and nothing
will keep them down. You aren't worried.
For you there is only more good land.

When You Speak to Me

Take care when you speak to me.
I might listen, I might
draw near as the flame
breathing with the log, breathing
with the tree it has not
forgotten. I might
put my face
next to
your face
in your nameless trouble,
in your trouble
and name.

It is a thing I learned
without learning; a hand
is a stronger mouth, a kiss could
crack the skull, these
words, small steps
in the air calling
the secret hands, the mouths
hidden in the flesh.

This isn't robbery.
This isn't your blood for my
tears, no confidence
in trade or barter. I may
say nothing back
which is to hear
after you the fever
inside the words we say
apart, the words we say so hard
they fall apart.

A Poem in Translation

After years smuggling poems
out of an unknown country,
you have been discovered by a known
and skillful master. Your language
is foreign and eligible, your circumstances
Russian, complete with prison camps
and midnight journeys by train
through the Urals. Someone is always taking
your hand as a stranger, entrusting you
with a few saved belongings
before he is led away.

You too are led, a pair of eyes
wearing sight like an armor.
You witness it all. You do not suffer
the physical shame, your clothes
taken from you, your body
made to stand with the weeping others.
Somehow you are not harmed.
You stitch a cry into the hem of your coat
to be unraveled in a land of comfort.

They work over the lines like a corpse
taken from the ground. Gradually
they heap their own flesh
over what has remained,
the beautiful gaps and silences.

In the new language you are awkward.
You don't agree with yourself,

these versions of what you *meant*
to say. Like a journalist, one has written
"throat" where you have said
"throat." Another uses his ears
as a mouth; he writes like an orator
in a bathroom, not "tears"
but "sobbing."

Still another has only heard your name
and the title of one poem
full of proper names, rivers
and cities no one bothers
to translate. All his poems begin here
and move into the dream of you
as the ideal sacrifice, redeeming him
from a language he knows too well
to say anything simply.

One night (it always happens at night)
these translations, against all precautions,
are smuggled back to you by a woman
looking much like yourself. She
takes your hand and leads you away
into a room where each one calls you
by his name and you enter the solitary
kingdom of your face.

Stepping Outside

for Akhmatova

Hearing of you, I never lost a brother
though I have, never saw a husband to war,
though I have, never kept with my father
the emptiness of his hands, my mother
the dying of her womb.

Return: husbands, sons, fathers return.
Many with both arms, with dreams
broken in both eyes.
They try, they try
but they cannot tell us
what comes back with them.

One more has planted his hoe
in my heart like an axe, my farmer uncle
slain by thieves
in the night, burned down
with his house, buried, dug up
to prove he was no dog.
He was no dog.

You, who lived in your pain until it grew
its own face, would have left all this
like a monument in a field. Your words
would have made a feast of what ate you.

Sit with me.
No one has left; no one returns.

Time Lapse with Tulips

That kiss meant to sear my heart forever –
it went right by.
And the way we walked out on Sundays
to the bakery, like a very old couple, arm
on arm, that's gone too
though the street had a house with a harp
in the window.

Those tulips again.
They think if they keep being given away
by the black-haired man at our wedding
I will finally take them in time
for the photograph. But they are wrong.
This time I will hand them back or leave them
sitting in the Mason jar
on the grass beside you.

See how the guests lean after me, their mouths
slightly open. Only now it's plain
they were never sure, that the picture
holding us all preserves
a symmetry of doubt with us
at the center, the pledge
of tulips red against my dress.

Whatever the picture says, it is wrong.
I take my image back, the white
petals that were standing a while at your side,
petals falling a while

at your side. Here instead,
the trick of flesh held again to your cheek.
Inside, the rare bone of my hand and that harp
seen through a window suddenly so tempting

you must rush into that closed room, you must
tear your fingers across it.

Croce e Delizia al Cor

Remember, and already the lapse in
vision pulls you back
too suddenly, the swing lowering
the boughs of the ash. You could sail forever
through the side of some fundamental right
you were giving yourself
at his expense.

The swing repeats the arc, the air
under you. Crouched
in a moving corner, this looking down
makes you feel specially weighted for falling,
an urge to get between assassinations
of either fixity, sky or ground.

Where you tempt the arc to be happy on its own,
the baby's buggy careens down cloudless skies
breaking your eyeglasses, both lenses at
once. So the frame presents the eyes
in a harmony not understood as the harbor
falls away through ships.

This necessity of returns
prolongs everything. The tree belongs to the
lawn, though the swing, it's true, is artificial,
heading like that over the girl in braids
eating a peanut butter sandwich near
the fence. She is inventing her turn
while the parents rub up against
our house in a paroxysm of bad advice. They
would praise the swing if it subdued
the tree. And yes, because you didn't look away,
something was settled.

Just then your mother steps out
of the lilac, meaning to leave you
with a last word. Call it a continuous hesitation,
her not wanting to admit pain which demands
credit and balance. "Anyone, after all, can let things
go to hell," before the sun
smashes the horizon and you catch sight of the
buggy hurtling impossibly through an entire
generation of good intentions.

The harbor yawns in and
out. Behind, into branches, the nest
is a sky broken from you. It matches that holding
the ships just above water.
Even so, the baby will drown there on the lawn
with the broken lenses, the blur of intimate
conjunctions: that bird dying into the sweep of
your knees above the houses.

The Calm

We were walking through the bees
and stars. Our mouths
made a sense without us.
I loved your hands
because of your mouth, each star
because of a life not chosen
by the hand. I told you,
don't say it, the loss
of our lives beyond us. You
said it. You said it
for the sake of a loneliness
together, for the praise of our eyes
going on without shadows.

Even now, when all our nights
have washed away
and the apples have left
the trees, I am keeping your place
where the high grass
has entered the song. Like a swarm,
the heart moves with its separate
wings under the eaves.

If I knew where to find you
I would say goodbye
and have the hurtful ease of that,
but the gates are everywhere
and this calm – an imagined forgiveness,
the childhood before we meet again.

Corona

Personable shadow, you follow me into this
daylight-dream, the one even my body
knows nothing of.

This flesh is your halo, the meat you drag daily
across the earth like an injured
wife. The sun

surrounds us as the heart surrounds
the body. Let us
navigate each pleasure, each pain

like a doorway, its ambush: the mouth, the bouquet,
the six-story ladder, that
memory of a train

missed in Budapest, everything passing through.
The tail of a shirt
caresses the back of my brother who falls again

from the tractor in 1957. A woman's body
flies out of the house
like an insult. It is the day we are found

missing. See
the windows floating beside us into the next world,
admitting they don't know what they're for.

I will speak to you like a lover, not as one
I have used
to keep from being true. This water is a memory

of sleep folding us
under. Your face
covers mine; the moon of your face blasted from a train

through faults of light in the trees – again and
again cut off, this water
taking up our hands.

Zero

Stupid tranquility, to be most sure
in the abstract, the zebra
raising its head from the river, the clock
wound to the usual multitude, the junco bird
appearing as a miracle on the blind magician's
balcony. A thing among things,
the magician is there as an absolute, his
long sleeves, an attitude of sight
that amounts to seeing, the morning steady

in the orange grove. To sit with him
is to sense the luminous sides
of objects making a finite path
to an infinite doorway. See how he multiplies
himself like the doves in his hat,
not flying away into the village
but resting in the white brocade
on the crook of his arm.

He walks the promenade, a procession
of explicit consequences, the funeral
climbing the hill with its tub
of roses. Magic powder clings
to his tongue, alum and ginger. A mild
contraction in the landscape, his reticence
to prove himself. Doesn't the sun
look as if it got there again
over the handkerchief snake
in his palm? This knot could make you cry,

how it slips past itself, now a
bracelet, now a white stem
drawn in the serious air of your breath,
letting itself down, the careful
ballerina closing the halo
of her partner's arms.

Snowheart

In our houses, the snow keeps us
traveling. It says: your life
is where you are. The phone,
all day ringing by itself
over the next lot, isn't for you.

The man with the perfect
haircut makes a track
across the lawn, holding
his books like a
breast. *Snowheart*

you have said: *don't cut your black hair.*

Love's the only debt.
He's up again
and riding the best mare
ten miles by moonlight, the
spruce-backed fiddle
under his arm.

"Dance us the next one too.
If day comes, don't
tell. Let the horse
go home alone."

Snowheart. Someone's horse
circles the near house.
There is snow
on its back.

Rhododendrons

Like porches they trust their attachments,
or seem to, the road and the trees
leaving them open from both sides.
I have admired their spirit,
wild-headed women of the roadside,
how exclusion is only something glimpsed,
the locomotive dream that learns to go on
without caring for the landscape.

There is a spine in the soil
I have not praised enough:
its underhair of surface
clawed to the air. Elsewhere each shore
recommends an ease of boats, shoulders
nodding over salmon
who cross this sky with our faces.

I was justifying my confusion
the last time we walked this way.
I think I said some survivals need
a forest. But it was only the sound
of knowing. Assumptions
about roots put down like a deeper foot
seemed dangerous too.

These were flowers you did not cut,
iris and mums a kindness enough.
Some idea of relative dignities, I suppose,
let us spare each other; I came away
with your secret consent and this
lets you stand like a grief
telling itself over and over.

Even grief has instructions,
like the boats gathering light
from the water and the separate
extensions of the roots. So remembering
is only one more way of being alone
when the voice has gone everywhere
in the dusk of the porches
looking for the last thing to say.

II

from

UNDER STARS

What Cathál Said

*"You can sing sweet
and get the song sung
but to get to the third dimension
you have to sing it
rough, hurt the tune a little. Put
enough strength to it
that the notes slip. Then
something else happens. The song
gets large."*

Words Written Near a Candle

If I could begin anything
I'd say stop asking forgiveness, especially
theirs which was always
the fault mentioned in your condition.

Nettles could be feathers
the moment they brush your
ankle. At the same time: floods, earthquakes,
the various slaveries
hunchbacked near the fence
to catch your glance.

What is it to say that among the hired boats
we carried our bodies well, cracked
jokes, left the gaps
in our lives and not
the page? This far to learn
the boat does not touch the water!

And if this is goodbye,
it is a light nowhere near believing
and I am happy
and it is all right to make a distance
of a nearness, to say, "Boat, I have left you
behind. Boat,
I am with you."

Women's Tug of War at Lough Arrow

In a borrowed field they dig in their feet
and clasp the rope. Balanced
against neighboring women, they hold
the ground by the little gained
and leaning like boatmen rowing into
the damp earth, they pull
to themselves the invisible waves, waters
overcalmed by desertion
or the narrow look trained to a brow.

The steady rain has made girls of them,
their hair in ringlets. Now they haul
the live weight to the cries
of husbands and children, until the rope
runs slack, runs free
and all are bound again by the arms
of those who held them, not until, but so
they gave.

Four Dancers at an Irish Wedding

It was too simple and too right,
the father blue-eyed
and doting, his daughter a mock-up
of the bride in her long dress, earrings
and matching steps.

Red shirt, I am right
for you, wrong for you. Here
is my cheek forever
in this careless waltz
where we chanced to meet.

Darling, darling, darling

in the sob-throated beat
and we are true, my sad-eyed partner,
truest to complicate the step, taking
this father's hand, this child's.

The circle opens and closes
where our joined hands meet. Sweet
gladness, I
am not yours
and you are not mine. Break. Break
where the beat widens, take
the worried girl, leave me
the father.

Darling, darling, darling

we are all stolen and grieving
in the tender arms.
I have seen the magpie in the morning

on the back of a cow
singing: One
is for sorrow. One
is for sorrow.

Drop the strange hand, be
lifted, child, held
there on your father's swaying shoulder
for we are one and one and
one with ourselves
on the polished floor.

The Ritual of Memories

When your widow had left the graveside
and you were most alone
I went to you in that future
you can't remember yet. I brought
a basin of clear water where no tear
had fallen, water gathered like grapes
a drop at a time
from the leaves of the willow. I brought
oils, I brought a clean white gown.

"Come out," I said, and you came up
like a man pulling himself out of a river,
a river with so many names
there was no word left for it but 'earth'.

"Now," I said, "I'm ready. These eyes
that have not left your face
since the day we met, wash these eyes.
Remember, it was a country road
above the sea and I was passing
from the house of a friend. Look
into these eyes where we met."

I saw your mind go back through the years
searching for that day and finding it,
you washed my eyes
with the pure water
so that I vanished from that road
and you passed a lifetime
and I was not there.

So you washed every part of me
where any look or touch
had passed between us. "Remember,"

I said, when you came to the feet,
"it was the night before you would ask
the girl of your village to marry. I
was the strange one. I was the one
with the gypsy look.
Remember how you stroked these feet."

When the lips and the hands
had been treated likewise and the pit
of the throat where one thoughtless kiss
had fallen, you rubbed in the sweet oil
and I glistened like a new-made thing, not
merely human, but of the world gone past
being human.

"The hair," I said. "You've forgotten
the hair. Don't you know it remembers.
Don't you know it keeps everything. Listen,
there is your voice and in it the liar's charm
that caught me."

You listened. You heard your voice
and a look of such sadness
passed over your dead face that I wanted
to touch you. Who could have known
I would be so held? Not you
in your boyish cunning; not me
in my traveler's clothes.

It's finished.
Put the gown on my shoulders.
It's no life in the shadow of another's joys.
Let me go freely now.
One life I have lived for you. This one
is mine.

As If It Happened

She was brought up manly for a woman
to dread the tender word.
All afternoon saying goodbye
in the high-ceilinged room, he
in the rocker, its fixed
reach, the whiskey troubling
their glasses.

The dull pull of the light fanned
and narrowed between them.
She had on the red handkerchief shirt.
They talked, the memory of that, two
made fearless and humble
as those who visit the dying, their live gifts
that need tending.

Say of them: "They were lovers once"
though little stays of that.
Yet didn't the body speak? Didn't it
fly out of its heart, its faithless
goldfish of a heart? Didn't it find your house,
opened by moonlight, walking up to it,
like a masterpiece of regret: only arms, only
the bodies of so many kisses
loosed like birds against the windows, falling.

And if that night happened, if one night
I walked up to your house shared by then
with another, wouldn't you
know me? Wouldn't you
remember one night when we were holy and helpless
in each other and wouldn't you start up then
like one in terror who has dreamed himself

backwards, dreaming he could not help stepping out
at the wrong and irrevocable moment – you
stepped out.

Now they're past recalling
and that night revolves like a planet forsaken
of its days and years. Of the two
who can tell which now
is retreating, which
has stepped this way?

On Your Own

How quickly the postures shift.
Just moments ago we seemed human,
or in the Toledo of my past
I made out I was emotionally illiterate
so as not to feel a pain I deserved.

Here at the Great Southern
some of the boys have made it
into gray suits and pocket calculators.
I'm feeling end-of-season, like a somebody
who's hung around the church
between a series of double weddings.

Friend, what you said about the terror
of American Womanhood,
I forget it already, but I know
what you mean. I'm so scary some days
I'd run from myself. It's hard work
having your way, even
half the time, and having it,
know what not to do with it. Who
hasn't thrown away a life or two
at the mercy of another's passion,
spite or industry.

It's like this on your own: the charms
unlucky, the employment
solitary, the best love always
the benefit of a strenuous doubt.

Woman-Enough

Figures on a silent screen,
they move into my window, its facing
on the abbey yard, six men with spades
and long-handled shovels. I had looked up
as I look up now across the strand where a small boat
has drifted into the haze of mountains
or that child walks to the end
of a dock.

Both views let in sun.
The bearded one throws off his coat
and rolls his sleeves. Two in their best clothes
from offices in London lean against a stone,
letting the shovels lift and slap.
The others dodge in and out of sun, elbow-high,
the ground thickening. The boat,
closer, one oar flashing,

pulled to the light and under, these voices
a darker blade. A wind
carries over and I hear him call out to me: "He
was a wild one in his young days. You'll want
to lock your door." He nods the bottle
to bring me out.

A drink to you, Peter Harte, man
that I never knew, lover
of cattle and one good woman
buried across the lake.
"He was a tall man, about my size," the one
measuring, face down in the gap.
"And wouldn't you like a big man? Big
as me?" dusting his hands on his pants and lifted out.

"Try it on, go down."

The sky, the stone blue
of the sky. An edge of faces, hard looks
as though they'd hauled me live
into the open boat of their deaths, American woman,
man-enough in that country place
to stand with skulls sifted and stacked
beside the dirt pile, but woman then
where none had stood and them more men
for that mistake to see me
where he would lay.

"Not a word of this to Mary, ye hear."

O he was a wild one,
a wild one in his youth. Sonny Peter
Harte.

The Ballad of Ballymote

We stopped at her hut
on the road to Ballymote
but she did not look up
and her head was on her knee.

What is it, we asked.
As from the dreams of the dead
her voice came up.

My father, they shot him
as he looked up from his plate
and again as he stood and again
as he fell against the stove
and like a thrush his breath
bruised the room
and was gone.

A traveler would have asked directions
but saw she would not lift her face.
What is it, he asked.

My husband sits all day in a pub
and all night and I may as well
be a widow for the way he beats me
to prove he's alive.

What is it, asked the traveler's wife,
just come up to look.

My son's lost both eyes in a fight
to keep himself a man
and there he sits behind the door
where there is no door

and he sees by the stumps
of his hands.

And have you no daughters for comfort?

Two there are and gone to nuns
and a third to the North
with a fisherman.

What are you cooking?

Cabbage and bones, she said. Cabbage
and bones.

Disappearances in the Guarded Sector

When we stop where you lived, the house
has thickened, the entry
level to the wall with bricks, as though
it could keep you out.

Again the dream has fooled you into waking
and we have walked out
past ourselves, through the windows
to be remembered in the light
of closed rooms
as a series of impositions
across the arms of a chair, that woman's face
startled out of us so it lingers
along a brick front.

You are leading me back to the burned arcade
where you said I stood with you
in your childhood last night, your childhood
which includes me now
as surely as the look of that missing face
between the rows of houses.

We have gone so far into your past
that nothing reflects us.
No sun gleams from the glassless frame
where a room burned,
though the house stayed whole. There
is your school, your church,
the place you drank cider at lunch time.
New rows of houses are going up.
Children play quietly in a stairwell.

Walking back, you tell the story
of the sniper's bullet
making two clean holes in the taxi, how
the driver ducked and drove on
like nothing happened. No pain
passed through you; it
did not even stop the car
or make you live more
carefully. Near the check point we
stop talking, you let the hands
rub your clothes
against your body. You seem to be
there, all there.

Watching, I am more apart
for the sign of dismissal they will give me,
thinking a woman would not conceal,
as I have, the perfect map
of this return where I have met
and lost you willingly
in a dead and living place.

Now when you find me next in the dream,
this boundary will move with us.
We will both come back.

Belfast. Winter, 1976

Open Fire Near a Shed

In the cab there was a song.
Not one I would have chosen, but
of which I remember, in my way,
some words without the tune. Also,
the driver, his coat. How is it
that the wrinkles in his coat-back
were almost tender? His small hands
taking from yours
my belongings.

You're stepping back now
behind the gray slats
of the gate. Your hand, the right
one, lifts through
the fine rain, causing me
to look back at myself
as your memory – a constancy
with its troubled interior
under the rained-on glass.

Looking out, I've moved already
into thought. The tunnel
on the train gives and returns my face
flickering across the winter fields,
the fields – their soft holdings
of water, of cows breathing warmly
over the tracks of birds.

Sudden then as light to the pane –
an open fire near a shed,
wilder in the stubble and light rain
for how it seems intended
to burn there
though no one is standing by.

Love Poem to Be Read to an Illiterate Friend

I have had to write this down
in my absence and yours. These
things happen. Thinking
of a voice added
I imagine a sympathy outside us
that protects the message
from what can't help
being said.

The times you've kept
your secret, putting on
glasses or glancing into a page
with interest, give again
the hurt you've forgiven, pretending
to be one of us.
So the hope of love
translates as a series of hidden moments
where we like to think
someone was fooled
into it.

Who was I then
who filled these days
with illegible warnings: the marriages
broken, the land
pillaged by speculators, no word
for a stranger?

This island
where I thought the language was mine
has left me lonely
and innocent as you or that friend

who let you copy his themes
until the words became pictures
of places you would never go.

Forgive it then
that so much of after
depends on these, the words
which must find you
off the page.

Second Language

Outside, the night is glowing
with earth and rain, and you
in the next room take up
your first language.
All day it has waited
like a young girl in a field.
Now she has stood up
from the straw-flattened circle
and you have taken her glance
from the hills.

The words come back.
You are with yourself again
as that child who gave up the spoon,
the bed, the horse to its colors
and uses. There is yet no hint
they would answer to anything else
and your tongue does not multiply the wrong,
the stammer calling them back
and back.

You have started the one word
again, again as though it had to be made
a letter at a time
until it mends itself into saying.
The girl is beside you as lover or mother or
the aunt who visited with a kindly face
and the story of your mother
as a girl in a life before you.

She leads you across that field
to where the cows put down their wet lips

to the rust-dry trough.
But before you can get there
it will have changed. The water
will have two names
in and out of the ground. The song
you are singing, its familiar words and measures,
will be shadowed and bridged.

Remember the tune for the words.
Remember the cows for the field, those
in their sacred look who return
their great heads to the centuries of grass.

Out of sleep you are glad
for this rain, are steadied by my staying awake.
The trough will fill
and it will seem as though the dream
completes its far side.

To speak is to be robbed and clothed,
this language always mine
because so partly yours. Each word
has a crack in it to show the strain
of all it holds, all that leaks
away. Silent now, as when another
would think you sullen or
absent, you smoke after a meal, the sign
of food still on the plate, the two
chairs drawn away and angled again
into the room.

The rain enters, repeating its single word
until our bodies in their store-bought clothes

make a sound against us, the dangerous visit
of the flesh perfecting its fears
and celebrations, drinking us in
by the slow unspeakable syllables.

I have forced up the screen
and put out the palm of my hand past the rush
of the eaves. In the circular glow of the porch
the lighted rain is still, is falling.

Still Moment at Dun Laoghaire

for Stevie

You cross the ramp, its sure suspension
above the blue rope net
that means water not seen
for this nearness of ship to dock.
Now it is below you, a channel
you will think of as an ocean
where we met once and talked back
into a lost continent, childhood,
and a single house that keeps us sisters.

You were right to call it a language,
the way I will know that tree
blocking the view of the peninsula
and the bluff dropping away each year
so the house must stand with conviction
flanked by the blue spruce, the swing set
waiting for our brothers' children.

Already we are more together
for how the house looks back on us.
Through the glass your face will float away
like a ship of its own
over the boundary that knows with us
the world is steady
in another view.

Look back. There is a woman
beside me, younger, older, waving
as you are waving yet,
with your blonde hair
wound and pinned, into this distance.

Ever After

Exactly like a rain cloud
over the picnickers at the abbey
or a boat reflecting
on the peak of itself without an oar, so
my death reached everything in my mind
effortlessly.

This amazed my normal appearance,
which went on swallowing
an excessive quantity of rain. An odd
expression of joy. Great sheets
of rain. Then passing

I caught the words of the mourners
like a skirt waving backwards on a scarlet road
and among them, the girl who would lay
beside me.

The long-handled shovel
from dawn to dark like a machine
and she one soft touch
for the gulls to swoop at. Cloth
buttons.

We looked at the red lights
wandering over the masts of the ships,
their dark facings in the brain,
the trees climbing side by side
with the sky into that exchange of worlds, her
hair flowing over
the river-wall. Her life, she said,

an imaginary bird let go in the white water
of January. Water that lapped

the doorstep, her short legs, her hand
on the window sill near the bridge, near
the look of the gulls
floating between the timbers.

Closing the fact of it, think
of her dead, think of a skeleton
you could embrace as the lack
of your being or lying
in this field to talk through the cry of water
into the whole future
which brings back the hands
free and ready. Think

of her. That's better. She
was at my side, the memory of her. The
wetness of the sea. I
explained to her: because you are alive
the horizon recedes. You thought you were
everything, a drum with affection, the sort
of girl to mark that page
because one hand held another
or you could skip it altogether.

If I were everything, there would be nothing
beside me. You
are beside me. The sort of girl
she was, looking out at me
through the lattices
of her hair, her
live hair.

Under Stars

The sleep of this night deepens
because I have walked coatless from the house
carrying the white envelope.
All night it will say one name
in its little tin house by the roadside.

I have raised the metal flag
so its shadow under the roadlamp
leaves an imprint on the rain-heavy bushes.
Now I will walk back
thinking of the few lights still on
in the town a mile away.

In the yellowed light of a kitchen
the millworker has finished his coffee,
his wife has laid out the white slices of bread
on the counter. Now while the bed they have left
is still warm, I will think of you, you
who are so far away
you have caused me to look up at the stars.

Tonight they have not moved
from childhood, those games played after dark.
Again I walk into the wet grass
toward the starry voices. Again, I
am the found one, intimate, returned
by all I touch on the way.

The Meeting

for Ken Schar

My name is not my own
and you are lost in the sameness
of yours: marriage, divorce,
marriage, the name changed
like a billboard at the side of my life.

That day I saw you last
you were wearing a white suit
in the mid-winter haze.
It was too big for you.
Your shoulders didn't belong.
I heard you: "If you feel
the rightness of a thing, do it."

Twelve years we've come
and not a word between us.
Last night you got off a bus
in my dream. Your body
seemed too small for itself. It was
hurt by something outside my sleep.
You took off your coat.
I could see the bones of your arms.
We didn't mention it.
You asked for something ordinary
and wrong, vitamins, I think.

You had your camera on your chest
like a complicated doorknob.
You didn't open.
My hands came back
to me. I was awake in that last café

where I did not say *brother,* where
I stood apart from your sorrow
in my great young indifference.

Tired lives had run you out.
You were going away. "Let them
have their bastard courage!"
Your hands came back
to you. You touched me, that hand
out of the grave. Early
and late, this hour has closed
around us.

Harmless Streets

Many times a last time I will look
into this room like walking
fully clothed into a floodstream.
Under the candelabra in a hotel lobby or
on the train where the commuters ruffle
their papers, or standing in a corridor of
elevators, it will come before me
as though I could never leave.

When I came to you
like a woman who dressed herself in the morning,
who spread the fan of her hair
at night on your pillow, they were with us already,
those days we would live
out of what you had done alone.

You were the man of fear and omens
who cast his own death in the slant of a tree or
looking up, caused a star inside the head
to break from space, but more often
it was loss of the simplest talisman, expected,
a slight regret that could end all.

Mostly no one saw what was done. The dead
were unspectacular, scattered and inarticulate,
preferring to be handled and stepped over,
though at times they seemed to argue
among themselves, a continual racket about the beauty
of the universe or the piteousness of the human
voice, filling the ancient night
with their elaborate nostalgia.

Once there was no doubt. That one
was yours and you walked to him where he lay

and you took from his pockets
a picture, no wife or child, but an image of
himself. If he had raised up on one arm
and said in the language of the dying, "Take this.
Remember me," you would not have done less.
But no, the dead have no such rights and the living
are merciless, saying, "Lie down. Be counted."

Each day his eyes are opened on your wall
among the emblems that returned whole legions, no glad
survivors, but hostage to these harmless streets.
And I who did not see what was done
have seen him cut off at the neck, have heard him speak
full bodied. He is offended
there on your wall in his one death, in your one life.
He has changed his mind
and wants only to be forgotten, not entirely, no
just enough to surprise your continuing
pain. Pain that continues is not pain, outleaps

the body. That soldier
in the poster near the armchair
keeps running toward us extending his wing
of blood. It is too red. It is only the color
red. I have tried
to see it otherwise, but cannot.

You are right. What can I know, a woman
who was never there? Empathy, sad apron, I take you
on and off. In loving
it was the same. I almost
felt. Your pleasure was almost mine.

The white tree near the window
looks in on your bed, the flowered sheets

where I drift with the parachutes of the men
sinking into watery fields.
But what can I know? I
who may not be counted, womb
of your secret shame and silences:
companion, mourner, thief.

The Same Kiss After Many Years

Like a cat haunting the familiar porch,
it's found us again, we
who meet now only to hear
what didn't happen to us, but to them,
those two we sent away
into lives we wanted
to see happening to us.

They've done well for themselves, as
expected. He's an artist. His work
sells. She's aged, but well,
from her bones out, has
travel plans, time yet
to pick and choose.

We're fond of them, not
just parental. Who else would listen
to us as we were
and take the blame
with such sad-eyed equanimity? They
know better now, would do it
over if they could.

We love their fateful hesitations,
self-caresses, the glance
that tells us plainly
there are those who await
their reappearance elsewhere. We're
concerned not to have them
missed, so this will happen
painlessly, leaving us all
the better for it.

They'll go back refreshed, seeing
how little we amounted to. Good
they got out when they did.
Let them kiss now, in the old
impassioned way, and go about their
business. They do it well, that
independence with a touch
of remorse. You're right. They're
better than we ever were. Kiss me.
Let's forget them.

Backdrop With Lovers, 1931

She's wearing a cotton dress
and sits on his lap casually, her arm
swung around his neck, as though she knew
this would happen, that moment, his hand
on her breast. Now we're all caught out here
in eternity by their expression in the singular.
Things were franker then?
Then. What may not be,
stopped.

Just as a quiver overtakes the landscape,
so each friendly beginning
is a hazard of sweet faces, birds flushed suddenly
from the lilac. Or because your manner
years later chooses an utter hopefulness,
we're made unequal
as the crowd parted by a blind walker. We
step aside and the calm planet of his head glides by.
That moment our thoughts stare
back at us, the nearest face closed
deeply into space.

She, then seventeen, could listen
while singing – her small wrists. Softly,
the important act takes place
without us, and she is crone now
or dead where painted treetops edge the blur
reminding. All that – years, back yards, sunning
in a neck-tied halter on the cellar door, whole cemeteries
of hopefulness have broken from sight
before the shutter. "Hold still, hold it!" one voice

still trying to check our disappearance
between the makeshift stars. Behind them, the waves,
stylized, restless as party hats. Just looking
we are flying with multitudes
into their future, the open boat and backdrop
skimming into floodlights in the pines, where, where?
Your knowing not to ask.

My Mother Remembers That She Was Beautiful

for Georgia Morris Bond

The falling snow has made her thoughtful
and young in the privacy
of our table with its netted candle
and thick white plates. The serious faces
of the lights breathe on the pine boards
behind her. She is visiting
the daughter never close
or far enough away to come to.

She keeps her coat on, called into
her girlhood by such forgetting
I am gone or yet
to happen. She sees herself
among the townspeople, the country glances
slow with fields and sky
as she passes or waits
with a brother in the hot animal smell
of the auction stand: sunlight,
straw hats, a dog's tail
brushing her bare leg.

"There are things you know.
I didn't have to beg," she said, "for anything."

The beautiful one speaks to me
from the changed, proud face and I see
how little I've let her know
of what she becomes. Years
were never the trouble, or the white hair
I braided near the sea
on a summer day. Who

she must have been
is lost to me through some fault
in my own reflection and we will have to go on
as we think we are, walking for no one's sake
from the empty restaurant into the one color
of the snow – before us, the close houses,
the brave and wondering lights of the houses.

III

from

WILLINGLY

Sudden Journey

Maybe I'm seven in the open field –
the straw grass so high
only the top of my head makes a curve
of brown in the yellow. Rain then.
First a little. A few drops on my
wrist, the right wrist. More rain.
My shoulders, my chin. Until I'm looking up
to let my eyes take the bliss.
I open my face. Let the teeth show. I
pull my shirt down past the collarbones.
I'm still a boy under my breast spots.
I can drink anywhere. The rain. My
skin shattering. Up suddenly, needing
to gulp, turning with my tongue, my arms out
running, running in the hard, cold plenitude
of all those who reach earth by falling.

Unsteady Yellow

I went to the field to break
and to bury my precious things.
I went to the field
with a sack and a spade,
to the cool field alone.

All that he gave me
I dashed and I covered.
The glass horse, the necklace,
the live bird with its song, with
its wings like two harps –
in the ground, in the damp ground.

Its song, when I snatched it again
to air, flung it with light
over the tall new corn, its pure joy
must have reached him.

In a day it was back, my freed bird
was back. Oh now, what will I do,
what will I do with its song
on my shoulder, with its heart
on my shoulder when we come to
the field, to the high yellow field?

Bird–Window–Flying

If we had been given names to love
each other by, I would take this one
from you, bird flying all day
in my woodhouse. The door
is open as when you came
to it, into it, as space between branches. "Never
trust doors," you tell the window,
the small of your body flung
against the white bay.

At dusk when I walked in
with my armload of green alder,
I could see the memory of light
shining water through your wings. You
were gray with it. The window
had aged you with promises.
I thought the boats, the gulls
should have stilled you
by now. When I cupped

my hands in their shadows, warm
over the heartwings, I saw the skin
of light between my fingers
haloed and glowing. Three steps I
took with you, for
you, three light years traveling
to your sky, beak
and claw of you, the soft burr of flight
at my fingerbones.

If I take a lover for every tree, I
will not have again such an opening as

when you flew from me.
I have gone in to build my fire. All
the walls, all the
wings of my house are burning. The flames
of me, the long hair
unbraiding.

I Save Your Coat, But You Lose It Later

It was a coat worth keeping even with
you in no condition to keep track, your mind
important to things you were seeing out
the window. We had changed seats on the bus
so a little breeze could catch
our faces. The coat was back there in a spot
of sunlight, its leather smell
making a halo of invitation around it.

We got off near the planetarium and were
heading for stars. Just to make one eye do
the work of two and bring back ghost-light
was making us forgetful. Then I looked at
you, strange without your coat, which
I knew you loved and had paid
an incredible price for, as if you had tried
to buy something that would make you sorry.

The bus was worrying itself into traffic, its
passengers locked into destinations. I ran
with everyone until they stopped in their
seats. There was your coat, a big interruption
in everybody's destination. When I picked it up,
it scalded my hand like an unbearable red
I saw once on a woman coming toward me.

We had a forty-year reunion right there
on the street, as if the coat
had met us again in its afterlife. We were
that glad, hugging it between us. Then you put
it on and checked yourself in the store window
wearing yourself those moments to see forgiveness

take your shape, then catching in the light
of those walking through you. I suppose it was
gratitude, your wearing it with telescopes, me
putting my hand in your pocket, pretending to
rob you while you looked for the first time
at the four moons of Jupiter.

Some weeks later, you write your coat was
stolen after a long night of drinking and
music. They took all your money. You never
saw it again. I am in a state of mourning
for your coat which traveled with us that while
like a close relative concealing a fatal illness
in a last visit. I remember a heart doctor
who saved a man for ten hours so his wife
disappeared into hope and would not come back
and would not take her lips from his until
they wheeled him away. I make too much of this,
your coat, which, stolen or lost, did not belong
to me, which I never wore.

The Hug

A woman is reading a poem on the street
and another woman stops to listen. We stop too,
with our arms around each other. The poem
is being read and listened to out here
in the open. Behind us
no one is entering or leaving the houses.

Suddenly a hug comes over me and I'm
giving it to you, like a variable star shooting light
off to make itself comfortable, then
subsiding. I finish but keep on holding
you. A man walks up to us and we know he hasn't
come out of nowhere, but if he could, he
would have. He looks homeless because of how
he needs. "Can I have one of those?" he asks you,
and I feel you nod. I'm surprised,
surprised you don't tell him how
it is – that I'm yours, only
yours, etc., exclusive as a nose to
its face. Love – that's what we're talking about, love
that nabs you with "for me
only" and holds on.

So I walk over to him and put my
arms around him and try to
hug him like I mean it. He's got an overcoat on
so thick I can't feel
him past it. I'm starting the hug
and thinking, "How big a hug is this supposed to be?
How long shall I hold this hug?" Already
we could be eternal, his arms falling over my
shoulders, my hands not
meeting behind his back, he is so big!

I put my head into his chest and snuggle
in. I lean into him. I lean my blood and my wishes
into him. He stands for it. This is his
and he's starting to give it back so well I know he's
getting it. This hug. So truly, so tenderly
we stop having arms and I don't know if
my lover has walked away or what, or
if the woman is still reading the poem, or the houses –
what about them? – the houses.

Clearly, a little permission is a dangerous thing.
But when you hug someone you want it
to be a masterpiece of connection, the way the button
on his coat will leave the imprint of
a planet in my cheek
when I walk away. When I try to find some place
to go back to.

Devotion: That It Flow;
That There Be Concentration

My friend keeps kissing me goodbye, the kisses
landing, out of nervousness, on and about
the face. "Leave the mistakes in," Ives told
his conductor, handing him the new score.
So it feels good, these sudden lips jabbing the chin
and forehead. We couldn't repeat it if
we tried. Looking back to him from the train, I'll
wave, though not too long – like a soul heading into
the underworld – but more as one standing at
the beginning of the beginning, a faint
smile, or as with stage fright suffered inexplicably
in an orchard.
                        We're moving.
The card players in the club car look up
as though they could prevent countryside – but we're
slicing into marshland so surely, a river
gives way to hillside, the backs of houses, an iron
fence, the bricks of a factory where paper tubes
are made.
                Light falling into
        me. *Into*. Blades of light. Light
        with its own breath. So fast – the trees,
                                it moves the trees.

The porter has carried my suitcases.
Now he asks me how I want my coffee: "Black," I say,
"black and strong."
"Like me," he says, and it isn't a question.

It is mid-November and the first snow keeps arriving
between the tracks where the landscape stops briefly
at Providence. A bell rings. The iron wheels
shift for us. Snow, audible to the eyes, reconciles
endless variation. The tracks like a blank musical
score, running now beside us where the trees in clumps
dart up their sudden clefts.

> *Who's gone? Who's*
> *gone? Snowheart – where did you, into whose*
> *past go*
> *with only those particles of light*
> *exactly melting?*

I'm drinking coffee as we pass a child's camp –
a hatch of discarded boards. It is perched
like the abandoned nest of some enormous bird,
topping a bluff which carries as memory
into childhood where once we dug a house into
a hillside. The smell of earth fresh around us, dirt
sifting out of our sleeves beside our plates
at supper. We were the dead children, come home
to sit in goodness with the silence of our ghostly
parents. Now we are gone, and so are they, and where
I look up, the child's camp is a thicket the snow
has breathed on.

> Vision shaved away – the cords of my vision
> electric, sparked in the current of
> fast ditches, fast silos, chimneys that leap and
> dodge the banks. Water
> standing in yellow grass, leaves, a few
> left hanging, tortured so
> the words *defoliation* and *napalm* occur.

The opening pages of Malraux's *Lazarus*: mustard gas
drifting over the Russians in their trenches at Bolgako

until the Germans change their minds about killing
those they have already killed, take the dead
and half-living soldiers in their arms and
stumble back to lives never again the same.

Passing as another kind of dwelling.
        At night the mills are torches between
    the trees. The snow climbs up, floats
            under the blue
                dark. The tunnels
    of the rabbits quiver and loosen when
                the fur rushes through them.

ii

I have traveled like sky with water far below, an
interlocking of surfaces. Or does the water lift
when sky hints into infinity
that change is the only durable ghost? This powder
of moments sheds the difference. Each shift,
eccentric and willful, is recorded as surely as
the chambers of the heart record blood
that will pass again, asking from time to
time where the body is.

    Interior of my face in the window, axis
        with a darkening motion.
            The mind flies out
                into this unconcealing.
                    Shadows
                            I kissed.
    The rutted track of thought without
                purpose.

We arrive at Mystic, the mind feeling itself as surface
to steeple, lumberyard, old barrels, a newly built

set of steps heading for a second story: "Up!"
my sight says, until a door opens
and a child steps out
onto the landing.

iii

We pass over trains, then into a conflicting mesh
of wrecked machines. A gull appears like a fish
above an empty playground. Then *WALL,* its rushing: *WALL*
inches from my window, the eyes – their flesh
driven back into the body.

How many times we defy matter heading into the ground
until it rises to either side – shoots by as motion
suddenly delivered to hillside or the mind incarnate –
retaining each recent death at its most living point.

Lunch at Old Saybrook.
The elderly woman across from me reads her newspaper
with a magnifying glass. Something blue flashes by.
Blue catches
in the landscape for miles.

The woman has spread her coat across her knees.
She is asleep, or seems so. A graveyard near a river
startles no one's composure, though some
who didn't mean to be looking must see it, where,
in its stead, a yellow truck passes to a yellow house
we lose before woods again.

The woman is asleep and I think my seeing keeps
the world for her. I think of her
like a picnic table in winter, passively unanchored
by the season. I see IS
under her magnifying glass in the empty seat next to her.

At night the houses flicker
between the trees. Every light is the same face you
                cannot leave, saying: "I am not leaving,
                        though I kiss the last mouth, yours, even
                yours, without touching."

My eye roars its black blood across the snow-light. My
lantern swings me in a golden arc.
  Show-me-show-me: the dwarf flowers
              of their heads
          in the windows, in the night water.

Bless now
                each lit place where no one
will pass tonight, these yellow shrines, elbows
                        into the dark.

The porter wants to know what I've written.
I read it to him where he stands in the aisle, and
he says, "That's beautiful. Is that
what you do for a living?"
"Yes," I say, "for a living."

We pull into yet another station, and he pats my hand,
leans close. "You're lucky," he says, and I feel
all that has gotten away from me
in what he misses. When I step down
onto the platform, there is a train in my memory.
Memory which rushes to add itself
to the startling impression of future pouring in.

The sleeping woman stays with the train, sleeping on,
grave and constant as the silent towns arrive.

Not There

One whistle, a short husky breath –
like a child blowing into a metal pipe then
listening. The house shudders
as the train passes on the hillside.
Days, mornings – whatever I'm doing I stop
and rush to wave it by. But always
I'm too late for the engineer.
It's the man in the caboose
who's searched out my doorway.
His grave face and hand say *hello-goodbye*.

Other times the train is coming
and I don't go out. I go on
doing what I'm doing – reading, or staring
at the gulls rising and falling above
the waves. I don't
go out. A weight pulls
against the house. I think of his grave face
looking down at the house, of the woman
in the doorway. I don't go out and
I don't go out. These
are the moments when we meet.

Crêpes Flambeau

We are three women eating out
in a place that could be California
or New Jersey but is Texas and our waiter
says his name is Jerry. He is pink
and young, dressed in soft denim
with an embroidered vest and, my friend says,
a nice butt. It's hard not to be intimate
in America where your waiter wants
you to call him Jerry. So why
do you feel sorry for him
standing over the flames
of this dessert?

The little fans of the crêpes are
folding into the juice. The brandy
is aflare in a low blue hush and golden
now and red where he spills
the brown sugar saved
to make our faces wear the sudden burst. We
are all good-looking and older and he
has to please us or try
to. What could go wrong? Too much
brandy? Too little sugar? Fire
falling into our laps, fire
like laughter behind his back, even
when he has done it just right. "Jerry,"
we say, "that was wonderful," for now
he is blushing at us
like a russet young girl. Our lips

are red with fire and juice.
He knows we could go on
eating long into the night until the flames

run down our throats. "Thank you,"
he says, handing us our check, knowing
among the ferns and napkins that he has
pleased us, briefly, like all
good things, dying away
at the only moment, before
we are too happy, too
glad in the pioneer decor: rough boards,
spotted horses in the frame.

Conversation with a Fireman from Brooklyn

He offers, between planes,
to buy me a drink. I've never talked
to a fireman before, not one from Brooklyn
anyway. Okay. Fine, I say. Somehow
the subject is bound to come up, women
firefighters, and since I'm
a woman and he's a fireman, between
the two of us, we know something
about this subject. Already
he's telling me he doesn't mind
women firefighters, but what
they look like
after fighting a fire, well
they lose all respect. He's sorry, but
he looks at them
covered with the cinders of someone's
lost hope, and he feels disgust, he just
wants to turn the hose on them, they
are that sweaty and stinking, just like
him, of course, but not the woman he
wants, you get me? and to come to that –
isn't it too bad, to be despised
for what you do to prove yourself
among men
who want to love you, to love you,
love you.

Some with Wings, Some with Manes

Over the stone wall her hand comes,
each knuckle enlarged to a miniature
skull. She reaches into my rented yard
to call me neighbor. Sunlight dazzles
her spectacles, and in the chromium glint
of her walker she is bright royalty
on an errand of magnitude. An effort to
stand, an effort to step the pain
carefully around invisible parameters
and still to say: effort is nobility.

Her hands are perfectly good for pointing.
That small, bare tree near my walkway, if
pruned, would be heavy with peaches
the size of your fist by July. In new regard,
I think what it could and will do. Then, not
to demean its offering, keep the next thought –
that I'll be gone by summer.

She has the name of a workhorse
I knew in Missouri, Dolly, and has outlived
a sister lost to the same disease. "She
sat down with it and that was the end of
her." Such variations on reluctance
cause me to see a kite
stubborn in a childhood pear tree, still abash
in the wind with its complication
of branches. I sighted my days
by its banners, until the tree caressed it
into flight, one day I wasn't looking.

For didn't the memory of the tree go with
it, the shred of it, less articulate

by then, a slip of motion longing to wrap itself
in a tattered lunge at the whole air?
After that, the tree said only the same thing
other trees say before coming to fruit.
Somehow we knew in our child-hearts
when a thing is ruined, not to meddle
with ecstasy by setting it free. We left it,
though it ruffles the mind yet.

Sitting in the darkened afternoon of her
living room, I hear the death
of the only daughter, meet the husband
who loves eggs and sweets, says little.
"I'm the last of my family," she says, then,
in the walker, leads me down the grassy corridor
to a room sleeping like a princess. The spell,
I see, is in the elaborate coverlet.

She will teach me how to do it. "It
took me fourteen months of evenings,"
the hands now going out
to the stitched pieces, remembering they
have done this. I know I will never do it,
will be gone by summer. "What is it called?"
"Cathedral Windows," she says,
and the razed light of her hands
falls over me.

View from an Empty Chair

Late afternoon light between peach trees.
No movement. Just one child-voice
telling another, "I'll show you!" – then
heading into valor – sound of furious pedaling,
clash of spokes. A wash of sparrows
breathes from a rooftop where periscopes
of pipes and ducts cause the houses
to submerge in the deep air.

Behind me, the muzzle of a hound
snuffles the stone ledge. Mournfully, I
occur to him, an intonation of wrongness
in the landscape. I feel the danger I mean
to someone unknown and near.

Over the wall a coffee mug appears, then
upper torso. The woman lets the dog
bound against her. "He hates
men," she tells me. His soft, loose mouth
lunges against the guard-wire – proving
loyalty by insistence on threat.

She lives alone, has had tools
stolen from the patio. Visitors and
burglars chance the house dog, a terrier
I hear as *terror*. (The air
is finely tuned.) One glance away
and her head is gone.

Country western bleeds from a doorway
opened brightly to *there goes my
everything*, then shut so birds
come in as underscoring to a car

luffing past. My house, with quiet skill,
intends to pull over me
with shadow.

The child recurs, imitating death pains
as comic and reversible. Taking up
my sweater and waterglass, I catch hold
of a child's drawing the wind has carried
into the yard. It has a friendly aspect,
the mouth like a hammock, though the hands
are levers and the eyes – demented
and aslant. We brighten once before
the house drops over us.

Tableau Vivant

They think it's easy to be dead, those
who walk the pathway here in stylish shoes,
portable radios strapped to their arms,
selling the world's perishables, even
love songs. They think you just lie down
into dreams you will never tell anyone.
They don't know we still have plans, a yen
for romance, and miss things like hats
and casseroles.

As for dreams, we take up where the living
leave off. We like especially those
in which the dreamer is about to
fall over a cliff or from a bridge that
is falling too. We're only too glad
to look down on the river gorge enlarging
under a body's sudden weight, to have the ground
rushing up instead of this slow
caving in. We thrive on living out
the last precious memories of someone escaped
back into morning light.

Occasionally there's a message saying they want
one of us back, someone out there
feeling guilty about a word or deed
that seems worse because we took it as
a living harm, then died
with it, quietly. But we know a lot about
forgiveness and we always make these trips with
a certain missionary zeal. We get back
into our old sad clothes. We stand again
at the parting, full of wronged tenderness and
needing a shave or a hairdo. We tell them

things are okay, not to waste their lives
in remorse, we never held it
against them, so much happens that no one means.

But sometimes one of us gets stubborn, thinks
of evening the score. We leave them calling
after us, *Sorry, Sorry, Sorry,* and we don't
look back.

Reading Aloud

When the light was shutting down on you
I said, "Behind my home is a palace of mountains."
I wanted you to see them, regal
in their shawls of snow above the working houses
of the town. I told them to you
the way a mother tells death to a child, so it seems
possible to go there and stay, leaving everyone
behind, saying softly, "Everyone's coming,"
so it's only a little while alone.

You were slipping from our days
like an opposite ripeness, still clinging
to the light. Each time you guessed your way home
by the edges, I saw my own image
freed in the streets of your memory, my face
like a time traveler's, forever young,
and every place you touched gave way.

I called it my year of the blind.
I was working for your friend who lived
a blindness he was born to.
"What did he lose? Noises, that's all
he knows," you said, would have no comfort
or instruction.

Long days I read aloud to your friend
the words that are the fountain sounds of the mind
causing light to fall inside itself over
the missing shapes of the world. "What do you think
when I say 'wings'?" I asked once. "Angels,
birds," he said, and I saw he could fly
with either. Once, about diamonds,

"Their light – a hiss in the rain
when the cars pass."

But you were memory-taunted by what was left
of your sight – the face of a beautiful
gradeschool teacher marooned in your childhood.
You cried against her neck and were grown.

The day we set out for the mountains
I strapped your sleeping bag to your back.
The woman who would call you "husband"
bound up her long hair and said your name
each time you fell and got up, *David, David*.
When we came to the chasm where a moss-slick log
was the only bridge, we looked down for you
at the river stones, the water over
and over them.

She loved you too much and could not lead you.
I took your hand and put all my sight there,
balancing between trust and the swiftness
we could fall to, walking backwards
so my grip was steady. When the river-sound
rocked us to either side, I fell deeper
for how you gave up to me
and to the river where we walked
like two improbable Christs held up by the doubt
that is the body.
When I let your hand drop on the far side
and we sank in the earth, the habit
of thanks was in me. Who could go with us
after that, though they joined us?

When I think of you in the years that have
passed us, I see a river under you

and always you are walking
into the shouting light of water and again
the wet smell of cloth
as when someone has been lifted free
with their breath still in them.

I know your walking is the other side of courage
and has no regard, like the cold faces
of the mountains seen from a childhood window
when the house is empty, when
with our many hands we have rushed through the rooms,
adding darkness, adding the words *mother, father,*
and no one answers back.

From Dread in the Eyes of Horses

Eggs. Dates and camel's milk.
Give this. In one hour the foal will
stand, in two will run. The care then of
women, the schooling from fear, clamor
of household, a prospect of saddles.

They kneel to it, folded
on its four perfect legs, stroke
the good back, the muscles bunched at the chest.
Its head, how the will shines large in it
as what may be used to overcome it.

The women of the horses comb out
their cruel histories of hair only for
the pleasure of horses, for the lost mares
on the Ridge of Yellow Horses, their white arms
praying the hair down breasts ordinary

as knees. The extent of their power,
this intimation of sexual wealth. From dread
in the eyes of horses are taken their songs.
In the white forests the last free horses
eat branches and roots, are hunted like deer
and carry no one.

A wedge of light where the doorway opens
the room – in it, a sickness of sleep.
The arms of the women, their coarse
white hair. In a bank of sunlight, a man
whitewashes the house he owns – no shores, no
worlds above it and farther, shrill, obsidian,
the high feasting of the horses.

Death of the Horses by Fire

We have seen a house in the sleeping town
stand still for a fire and the others,
where their windows knew it,
clothed in the remnants of a dream
happening outside them. We have seen
the one door aflame in the many windows,
the steady procession of the houses
trembling in heat-light, their well-tended
yards, the trellis of cabbage roses scrawled
against the porch – flickering white, whiter
where a darkness breathes back.

How many nights the houses have burned through
to morning. We stood in our blankets
like a tribe made to witness
what a god could do.

We saw the house built again in daylight
and children coming from it
as what a house restores to itself in rooms
so bright they do not forget, even
when the father, when the mother
dies. "Kitchen of your childhoods!" we shout
at the old men alive on the benches
in the square. Their good, black eyes
glitter back at us, a star-fall
of homecomings.

Only when the horses began to burn
in the funnel of light hurrying in one place
on the prairie did we begin to suspect
our houses, to doubt at our meals
and pleasures. We gathered on the ridge

above the horses, above the blue smoke
of the grasses, and they whirled in the close
circle of the death that came to them, rippling in
like a deep moon to its water. With
the hills in all directions
they stood in the last of their skies
and called to each other to save them.

3 A.M. *Kitchen: My Father Talking*

For years it was land working me, oil fields,
cotton fields, then I got some land. I
worked it. Them days you could just about
make a living. I was logging.

Then I sent to Missouri. Momma
come out. We got married.
We got some kids. Five kids.
That kept us going.

We bought some land near the water.
It was cheap then. The water
was right there. You just looked out
the window. It never left the window.

I bought a boat. Fourteen footer.
There was fish out there then.
You remember, we used to catch
six, eight fish, clean them right
out in the yard. I could of fished to China.

I quit the woods. One day just
walked out, took off my corks, said that's
it. I went to the docks.
I was driving winch. You had to watch
to see nothing fell out of the sling. If
you killed somebody you'd
never forget it. All
those years I was just working
I was on edge, every day. Just working.

You kids. I could tell you
a lot. But I won't.

It's winter. I play a lot of cards
down at the tavern. Your mother.
I have to think of excuses
to get out of the house. You're
wasting your time, she says. You're wasting
your money.

You don't have no idea, Threasie.
I run out of things
to work for. Hell, why shouldn't I
play cards? Threasie,
some days now I just don't know.

Boat Ride

for Galway

Since my girlhood, in that small boat
we had gone together for salmon
with the town still sleeping and the wake
a white groove in the black water, black
as it is when the gulls are just stirring and
the ships in the harbor are sparked with lights
like the casinos of Lucerne.
That morning my friend had driven an hour
in darkness to go with us, my father
and me. There'd been an all-night party.
My friend's face so tired I thought, *Eskimo-eyes*.
He sighed, as if stretched out
on a couch at the back of his mind.

Getting the bait and tackle. What
about breakfast? No breakfast.
Bad luck to eat breakfast before fishing, but
good luck to take smoked salmon to eat
on the water in full sun. Was my friend's coat
warm enough? The wind can come up.
Loaning him my brother's plaid jacket.

Being early on the water, like getting first
to heaven and looking back through memory
and longing at the town. Talking little, and
with the low, tender part
of our voices; not sentences but
friendlier, as in nodding to one who already
knows what you mean.

Father in his rain-slicker – seaweed green over
his coat, over blue work shirt, over cream-

colored thermal underwear that makes a white V
at his neck. His mouth open so the breath
doesn't know if it's coming or going – like any
other wave without a shore. His mind
in the no-thought of guiding the boat.
I stare into the water folding
along the bow, *gentian* – the blue with darkness
engraved into its name, so the sound
petals open with mystery.

Motor-sound, a low burbling with a chuckle
revolving in the *smack smack* of the bow
spanking water. *You hear me, but you don't
hear me,* the motor says
to the fish. A few stars
over the mountains above the town.
I think *pigtails,* and that the water under us
is at least as high as those mountains, deep
as the word *cello* whispered under water –
cello, cello until it frees a greeting.

We pass the Coast Guard station, its tower
flashing cranky white lights beside
the barracks where the seamen sleep in
long rows. Past the buoy, its sullen red bell
tilting above water. All this time
without fishing – important to get out of
the harbor before letting the lines
down, not time wasted but time
preparing, which includes invitation and
forgetting, so the self is occupied freely
in idleness.

"Just a boat ride," my father says, squinting
where sun has edged the sky toward Dungeness

a hazy mix of violet and pink. "Boat ride?"
I say. "But we want salmon."
"I'll take cod, halibut, old shoes, anything
that's going," says my friend. "And you'll get
dogfish," my father says. "There's enough
dogfish down there to feed all Japan."
He's baiting up, pushing the double hooks
through the herring. He watches us
let the lines out. "That's plenty," he says,
like it's plain this won't come
to much.

Sitting then, nothing to say for a while,
poles nodding slightly. My friend, slipping
a little toward sleep, closes his eyes.
Car lights easing along Ediz Hook, some
movement in the town, Port of the Angels,
the angels turning on kitchen lights,
wood smoke stumbling among scattered hemlock,
burning up questions, the angels telling
their children to get up, planning the future
that is one day long.

"Hand me that coffee bottle, Sis," my father
says. "Cup of coffee always makes the fish
bite." Sure enough, as he lifts the cup,
my pole hesitates, then dips. I brace
and reel. "Damned dogfish!" my father says,
throwing his cigarette into the water. "How
does he know?" my friend asks. "No fight,"
I say. "They swallow the hook down
their gullets. You have to cut
the leader."

No sun-flash on silver scales when it
breaks water, but thin-bellied brown, shark-

like, and the yellow-eyed insignia
that says: *there will be more of us.*
Dogfish. Swallower of hooks, waster of hopes
and tackle. My father grabs the line, yanks
the fish toward the knife, slashes twice,
gashing the throat and underbelly so
the blood spills over his hand.
"There's one that won't come back," he says.

My friend witnesses without comment or
judgment the death and mutilation
of the dogfish. The sun is up. My friend
is wide awake now. We are all wide
awake. The dogfish floats away, and a tenderness
for my father wells up in me, my father
whom I want my friend to love and who intends,
if he must, as he will, to humor us, to keep
fishing, to be recorded in the annals
of dogfish as a scourge on the nation of
dogfish which has fouled his line, which is
unworthy and which he will single-handedly
wipe out.

When the next fish hits my friend's line
and the reel won't sing, I take out my
Instamatic camera: "That's a beautiful
dogfish!" I say. "I'll tell them in New York
it's a marlin," my friend says. I snap
his picture, the fish held like
a trophy. My father leans out of
the frame, then cuts the line.

In a lull I get him to tell stories,
the one where he's a coal miner in Ottumwa,
Iowa, during the Depression and the boss
tries to send the men into a mine where

a shaft collapsed the day before. "You'll
go down there or I'll run you out of
this town," the boss says. "You don't
have to run me. I'm not just leaving
your town, I'm leaving your whole goddamned
state!" my father says, and he turns
and heads on foot out of the town, some
of the miners with him, hitching from there
to the next work in the next state.

My father knows he was free
back there in 1935 in Ottumwa, Iowa, and he
means you to know you don't have to risk
your life for pay if you can tell the boss to
go to hell and turn your heel. What
he doesn't tell is thirty years on the docks,
not a day missed – working, raising
a family.

I unwrap smoked salmon sandwiches and we bite
into them. It is the last fishing trip
I will have with my father. He
is ready to tell the one about the time
he nearly robbed the Seminole Bank in
Seminole, Oklahoma, but got drunk
instead and fell asleep.
He is going to kill five more dogfish
without remorse; and I am going to
carry a chair outside for him
onto the lawn of the Evergreen Radiation
Center where he will sit and smoke
and neither of us feels like talking, just
his – "The sun feels good."
After treatments, after going back
to my sister's where he plays with her baby –

"There's my gal! Is the Kiss Bank
open?" – in the night, rising up in the dream
of his going to say, "Get my billfold," as if
even his belongings might be pulled into
the vortex of what would come.

We won't catch a single salmon that day.
No strikes even. My friend and I
will share a beer and reminisce in advance
about the wonderful dogfishing we had.
My father wipes blood from his knife
across his knee and doesn't
look up. He believes nothing
will survive of his spirit or body. His god
takes everything and will not be
satisfied, will not be assuaged by the hopes, by
the pitiful half-measures of the living.
If he is remembered, that too
will pass.

It is good then,
to eat salmon on the water, to bait the hook
again, even for dogfish, to stare back at
the shore as one who withholds nothing, who,
in the last of himself, cannot put together
that meaning, and need not, but yields in thought
so peacefully to the stubborn brightness of
light and water: we are awake with him
as if we lay asleep. Good memory,
if you are such a boat, tell me
we did not falter in the vastness
when we walked ashore.

Accomplishment

What not to do for him
was hardest, for the life left in us
argued against his going
like a moon banished in fullness, yet
lingering far into morning, pale
with new light, gradually a view of
mountains, a sea emerging – its prickly
channels and dark shelves
breeding in the violet morning. Ships too,
after a while. Some anchored, others
moving by degree, as if to leave without affront
this harbor, a thin shoal curved like an arm –
ever embracing, ever releasing.

He too was shaped to agreement, the hands
no longer able to hold, at rest
on the handmade coverlet. His tongue
arched forward in the open mouth where breath
on breath he labored, the task beyond all strength
so the body shuddered like a chill
on the hinge of his effort, then rose again.

After a time, we saw the eyes gaze upward
without appeal – eyes without knowing or need
of knowing. Some in the room began to
plead, as if he meant to take them with him,
and they were afraid. A daughter bent near,
calling his name, then gave her own,
firmly, like a dock he might swim or cling to.
The breath eased, then drifted momentarily,
considering or choosing, we did not know.

"At some point we have to let him go."

"I know," she said. "I know."

In the last moments the eyes widened and,
with the little strength left, he
strained upward and toward. "He had to be
looking *at* something. You don't look
at nothing that way." Not
pain, but some sharpening beyond
the visible. Not eagerness or surprise, but
as though he would die in time to intercept
an onrushing world, for which
he had prepared himself
with that dead face.

Black Silk

She was cleaning – there is always
that to do – when she found,
at the top of the closet, his old
silk vest. She called me
to look at it, unrolling it carefully
like something live
might fall out. Then we spread it
on the kitchen table and smoothed
the wrinkles down, making our hands
heavy until its shape against Formica
came back and the little tips
that would have pointed to his pockets
lay flat. The buttons were all there.
I held my arms out and she
looped the wide armholes over
them. "That's one thing I never
wanted to be," she said, "a man."
I went into the bathroom to see
how I looked in the sheen and
sadness. Wind chimes
off-key in the alcove. Then her
crying so I stood back in the sink-light
where the porcelain had been staring. Time
to go to her, I thought, with that
other mind, and stood still.

Candle, Lamp & Firefly

How can I think what thoughts
to have of you with a mind so unready?
What I remember most: you did not want
to go. Then choice slipped from you
like snow from the mountain, so death
could graze you over with the sweet
muzzles of the deer moving up from
the valleys, pausing to stare
down and back toward the town. But you
did not gaze back. Like a cut rose
on the fifth day, you bowed
into yourself and we watched the shell-
shaped petals drop in clumps, then,
like wine, deepen into the white cloth.

What have you written here on my sleep
with flesh so sure I have no choice
but to stare back when your face and
gestures follow me into daylight?
Your arms, too weak at your death
for embracing, closed around me and held,
and such a tenderness was mixed there
with longing that I asked, "Is it good
where you are?"

We echoed a long time in the kiss
that was drinking me – *daughter, daughter,
daughter* – until I was gone as when a sun
drops over the rim of an ocean, gone
yet still there. Then the dampness,
the chill of your body pulled from me
into that space the condemned
look back to after parting.

Between sleep and death
I carry no proof that we met, no proof
but to tell what even I must call dream
and gently dismiss. So does
a bird dismiss one tree for another
and carries each time the flight between
like a thing never done.
And what is proof then, but some trance
to kill the birds? And what are dreams
when the eyes open on similar worlds
and you are dead in my living?

Woodcutting on Lost Mountain

for Leslie and for Morris

Our father is three months dead
from lung cancer and you light another Camel,
ease the chainsaw into the log. You
don't need habits to tell us
you're the one most like him.
Maybe the least loved
carries injury farther into tenderness
for having first to pass through
forgiveness. You
passed through. "I think he respected me
at the end," as if you'd waited a lifetime
to offer yourself that in my listening.

"Top of the mountain!" your daughter cries.
She's ten, taking swigs with us
from the beer can in the January sun. We see
other mountain tops and trees forever.
A mountain *could* get lost in all this, right
enough, even standing on it, thinking this
is where you are.

"Remember the cabins we built when we were
kids? The folks logging Deer Park and
Black Diamond." My brother, Morris, nods,
pulls the nose of the saw into the air as a chunk
falls. "We built one good one. They
brought their lunches and sat with us
inside – Spam sandwiches on white bread,
bananas for dessert and Mountain Bars, white
on the inside, pure sugar on
the inside – the way they hurt your teeth."

Sawdust sprays across his knee, his face
closes in thought. "Those whippings." He
cuts the motor, wipes his forehead with an arm.
"They'd have him in jail today. I used to beg
and run circles. You got it worse because you
never cried. It's a wonder we didn't
run away." "Away to where?" I say. "There's no
away when you're a kid. Before you can get there
you're home."

"Once he took you fishing and left me
behind," my brother says.
"I drew pictures of you sinking
all over the chicken house. I gave you a head
but no arms. We
could go back today and there
they'd be, boats
sinking all down the walls."

His daughter is Leslie, named after our father.
Then I think – 'She's a logger's daughter,
just like me' – and the thought pleases as if
the past had intended this present. "You
didn't know you were doing it," I tell him,
"but you figured how to stay
in our childhood." "I guess I did. There's
nothing I'd rather do," he says, "than cut wood.
Look at that –" he points to stacks of logs
high as a house he's thinned from the timber –
"they're going to burn them. Afraid
somebody might take a good tree
for firewood, so they'll burn half a forest.
Damn, that's the Forest Service for you. Me –
I work here, they'll have to stop me."

Leslie carries split wood to the tailgate
and I toss it into the truck. We make
a game of it, trying to stack as fast
as her father cuts. "She's a worker,"
Morris says. "Look at that girl go.
Sonofagun, I wouldn't trade four boys for her.
No sir." He picks up the maul, gives a yell
and whacks down through the center of a block
thick as a man. It falls neatly into
halves. "Look at that! Now *that's* good wood.
That's beautiful wood," he says, like he
made it himself.

I tell him how the cells of trees
are like the blood cells of people, how trees
are the oldest organisms on the earth. Before
the English cut the trees off Ireland, the Irish
had three dozen words for green. He's impressed,
mildly, has his own way of thinking about trees.

Tomorrow a log pile will collapse
on him and he will just get out alive.

"Remember the time Dad felled the tree on us
and Momma saved us, pushed us into a ditch? It's
a wonder we ever grew up."

"One of the horses they logged with, Dick
was his name, Old Dick. They gave him
to Oney Brown and Dick got into the house
while everyone was gone and broke
all the dishes. Dishes – what could they mean
to a horse? Still, I think he knew
what he was doing."

Oney's wife, Sarah, had fifteen kids. She's
the prettiest woman I'll ever see. Her son,
Lloyd, took me down to the railroad tracks
to show me the dead hounds. "We had too many
so they had to shoot some." The hounds were
skeletons by then, but they haven't moved
all these years from the memory
of that dark underneath of boughs.
I look at them, stretched on their sides, twin
arches of bones leaping with beetles and
crawlers into the bark-rich earth. Skipper
and Captain – Cappy for short. Their names
and what seemed incomprehensible – a betrayal
which meant those who had care of you
might, without warning, make an end of you
in some godforsaken, heartless place. Lloyd spat
like a father between the tracks, took
my hand and led me back to the others.

Twenty years settles on the boys
of my childhood. Some of them loggers.
"It's gone," they tell me. "The Boom Days
are gone. We thought
they'd never end, there were
that many trees. But it's finished,
or nearly. Nothing but stumps
and fireweed now."

"Alaska," Morris says, "that's where the trees
are," and I think of them, like some lost tribe
of wanderers, their spires and bloodless blood
climbing cathedral-high into the moss-light
of days on all the lost mountains of
our childhoods.

Coming into the town we see the blue smoke
of the trees streaming like a mystery
the houses hold in common.
"Doesn't seem possible –," he says, "a tree
nothing but a haze you could
put your hand through."

"What'll you do next, after the trees are gone?"

"Pack dudes in for elk."

"Then what?"

"Die, I guess. Hell, I don't know, ask
a shoemaker, ask a salmon. . . .
Remember that time I was hunting and got lost,
forgot about the dark and me with no coat, no
compass? You and Dad fired rifles from the road
until I stumbled out. It
was midnight. But I got out. It's a wonder
I could tell an echo from a shot, I was so cold,
so lost. Stop cussing, I told the old man, I'm
home, ain't I? 'You're grown,' he kept saying,
'you're a grown man.'
I must be part wild. I must be part tree or part
deer. I got on the track and I was lost
but it didn't matter. I had to go where it led.
I must be part bobcat."

Leslie is curled under my arm, asleep.

"Truck rocks them to sleep," Morris says.
"Reminds me, I don't have a license for this

piece of junk. I hope I don't get stopped. Look
at her sleep! right in the middle of the day.
Watch this: 'Wake up honey, we're lost. Help me
get home. You went to sleep and got us lost.'
She must be part butterfly, just look at those eyes.
There – she's gone again. I'll have to carry
her into the house. Happens every time.
Watch her, we'll go up the steps and she'll be
wide awake the minute I open the door.
Hard to believe, we had to be carried into houses
once, you and me. It's a wonder we ever
grew up."

Tomorrow a log pile will collapse
and he'll just get out alive.

He opens the door. Her eyes start,
suddenly awake.

"See, what'd I tell you. Wide awake. Butterfly,
you nearly got us lost, sleeping so long.
Here, walk for yourself. We're home."

Some Painful Butterflies Pass Through

I saw the old Chinese men standing
in Nanjing under the trees where
they had hung their caged birds
in the early morning as though a cage
were only another branch that travels
with us. The bird revolves and settles,
moving its mind up and down the tree
with leaves and light. It sings
with the free birds – what else
can it do? They sit on the rungs
and preen or jit back and down and
back. But they are busy
and a day in the sky makes wings
of them. Then some painful butterflies
pass through.

The old men talk and smoke, examine
each other's cages. They feel restored,
as if they'd given themselves a tree, a sky
full of companions, song
that can travel. They depend
on their birds, and if their love stories
swing from their arms as they walk
homeward, it may be they are chosen
after all like one tree
with one bird that is faithful,
an injured voice traveling high into silence

with one accustomed listener
who smiles and walks slowly with
his face in the distance so
the pleasure spreads, and the treasured
singing, and the little bursts
of flying.

Shanghai. June 11, 1983

Gray Eyes

When she speaks it is like coming onto a grave
    at the edge of a woods, softly, so we
            do not enter or wholly
        turn away. Such speech
    is the breath a brush makes through hair,
            opening into time
        after the stroke.

            A tree is bending
    but the bird doesn't land.

            One star,
    earthbound, reports a multitude of unyielding
        others. It
            cannot help its   falling   falling
    into the dull brown earth of someone's back yard,
        where, in daylight, a hand reaches
    in front of the mower and tosses it, dead stone,
            aside. We who saw it fall

    are still crashing with light into the housetops,
        tracing in the mind that missing
            trajectory, rainbow of darkness
        where we were – children
    murmuring – "There, over there!" – while the houses
        slept and slept on.

    Years later she is still nesting on the light
        of that plundered moment, her black hair
            frozen to her head with yearning,
        saying, "Father, I am a colder green
            where the mower cut a swath
                and I lay down

and the birds that have no use for song
      passed over me
   like a shovel-fall."

She closed her eyes. It was early morning. Daybreak.
   Some bees
          were dying on my wing – humming
   so you could hardly hear.

Linoleum

for Mark Strand

There are the few we hear of
like Christ, who, with divine grace,
made goodness look easy, had
a following to draw near, gave up
the right things and saw to it
that sinners got listened to.
Sharpening my failures, I remember
the Jains, the gentle swoosh
of their brooms on a dirt path
trodden by children and goats, each
thoughtful step taken in peril of
an ant's life or a fat grub hidden
under a stick. In the car wash,
thinking of yogis under a tree
plucking hair by hair the head
of an initiate, I feel at least
elsewhere those able for holiness –
its signs and rigors – are at work.
Ignominiously, I am here, brushes
clamped, soap and water pulsing
against my car. (A good sign too,
those asylums for old and diseased
animals.) My car is clean
and no one has had to
lift a finger. The dead
bugs have been gushed away into a soup
of grit and foam – the evidence
not subterranean, but streaming along
the asphalt in sunlight so dazzling
I attend the birth-moment of
the word *Hosannah!*

I care about the bugs and not
in this life will I do enough towards
my own worth in the memory
of them. I appreciate the Jains,
their atonements for my neglect,
though I understand it makes poor farmers
of them, and good we all
don't aspire to such purity so
there's somebody heartless enough to
plow the spuds.

Early on, in admiration, I put off
knowledge, and so delayed reading about
the Jains – not to lose
solace. But in the county library,
turning a page, I meet them as
the wealthiest moneylenders
in Western India. Reading on,
I'm encouraged – the list of virtues
exceeds vices – just four
of those: anger, pride, illusion and
greed. The emphasis clearly on
striving. I write them down
in the corner of a map
of Idaho: forbearance, indulgence,
straightforwardness, purity,
veracity, restraint, freedom from
attachment to anything, poverty
and chastity.

Choosing, getting into the car to
get to the supermarket, hearing
over engine noise the bright agonies

of birds, the radio news with the child
nailed into a broom closet for
twenty-four hours by parents who
in straightforwardness sacrificed
forbearance, I feel a longing
for religion, for doctrine swift
as a broom to keep the path
clear. Later, alone in the kitchen
with the groceries, I read the list
again. Overwhelmed by the loneliness
of the saints, I take up my broom
and begin where I stand,
with linoleum.

Willingly

When I get up he has been long at work,
his brush limber against the house.
Seeing him on his ladder under the eaves,
I look back on myself asleep in the dream
I could not carry awake. Sleep
inside a house that is being painted,
whole lifetimes now only the familiar cast
of morning light over the prayer plant.
This "not remembering" is something new
of where you have been.

What was settled or unsettled in sleep
stays there. But your house
under his steady arm is leaving itself
and you see this gradual surface of
new light covering your sleep
has the greater power.
You think now you felt brush strokes or
the space between them, a motion
bearing down on you – an accumulation
of stars, each night of them
arranging over the roofs of entire cities.

His careful strokes whiten the web,
the swirl of woodgrain blotted
out like a breath stopped
at the heart. Nothing has changed
you say, faithlessly. But something has
cleansed you past recognition. When
you stand near his ladder looking up
he does not acknowledge you,
and as from daylight in a dream you see
your house has passed from you
into the blessed hands of others.

This is ownership, you think, arriving
in the heady afterlife of paint smell.
A deep opening goes on in you.
Some paint has dropped onto your shoulder
as though light concealed an unsuspected
weight. You think it has fallen through
you. You think you have agreed to this,
what has been done with your life, willingly.

Each Bird Walking

Not while, but long after he had told me,
I thought of him, washing his mother, his
bending over the bed and taking back
the covers. There was a basin of water
and he dipped a washrag in and
out of the basin, the rag
dripping a little onto the sheet as he
turned from the bedside to the nightstand
and back, there being no place

on her body he shouldn't touch because
he had to and she helped him, moving
the little she could, lifting so he could
wipe under her arms, a dipping motion
in the hollow. Then working up from
the feet, around the ankles, over the
knees. And this last, opening
her thighs and running the rag firmly
and with the cleaning thought
up through her crotch, between the lips,
over the V of thin hairs –

as though he were a mother
who had the excuse of cleaning to touch
with love and indifference
the secret parts of her child, to graze
the sleepy sexlessness in its waiting
to find out what to do for the sake
of the body, for the sake of what only
the body can do for itself.

So his hand, softly at the place
of his birth-light. And she, eyes deepened

and closed in the dim room.
And because he told me her death as
important to his being with her,
I could love him another way. Not
of the body alone, or of its making,
but carried in the white spires of trembling
until what spirit, what breath we were
was shaken from us. Small then,
the word *holy*.

He turned her on her stomach
and washed the blades of her shoulders, the
small of her back. "That's good," she said,
"that's enough."

On our lips that morning, the tart juice
of the mothers, so strong in remembrance, no
asking, no giving, and what you said, this
being the end of our loving, so as not to hurt
the closer one to you, made me look
to see what was left of us
with our sex taken away. "Tell me," I said,
"something I can't forget." Then the story of
your mother, and when you finished
I said, "That's good, that's enough."

IV

NEW POEMS

What sort of times are these?
And who has a clear conscience?

Eat, drink and be thankful! –
But how can I do this
If my food belongs
To the starving
My drink to the parched?

At the same time, I eat and drink.

DEREK MAHON, "Brecht in Svendborg"

If Poetry Were Not a Morality

It is likely I would not have devoted myself to poetry in this world
which remains insensitive to it, if poetry were not a morality.

JEAN COCTEAU, *Past Tense*

I'm the kind of woman who
when she hears Bobby McFerrin sing without words
for the first time on the car radio has to
pull over and park with the motor
running. And Cecil Taylor, I pulled over
for him too, even though later the guy
at the record store said he was just
a 'side man.' Something he did with silence and
mixing classical with I'm-worried-about-this-but-I-
have-to-go-this-way-anyhow. *This* not letting me
go. What did you do, the guy asked me, when you
pulled over? Smiled, I said, sat

and smiled. If the heart could be that simple. The photo
of Gandhi's last effects taped near
my typewriter: eyeglasses, sandals, writing paper
and pen, low lap-sized writing desk and something
white in the foreground like a bedroll.
Every so often I glance at this, just paper torn
from a book, and wish I could get down to
that, a few essentials, no
more. So when I left this place it would be
humbly, as in those welfare funerals my mother
used to scorn because the county always bought

the cheapest coffins, no satin lining, and if you
wanted the dead to look comfortable
you had to supply your own

pillow. I still admire her hating to see the living
come off cheap in their homage to any life. She
was Indian enough so the kids used to
taunt me home with "Your mother's a squaw!"
Cherokee, she said. And though nobody
told me, I knew her grandfather had to be
one of those chiefs who could never

get enough horses. Who if he had two hundred
wanted a hundred more and a hundred more
after that. Maybe he'd get up in the night and go
out among them, or watch their grazing
from a distance under moonlight. He'd pass his mind
over them where they pushed their muzzles into
each other's flanks and necks and their horseness
gleamed back at him like soundless music until
he knew something he couldn't know
as only himself, something not to be told again
even by writing down the doing

of it. I meet him like that sometimes,
wordless and perfect, with more horses than he
can ride or trade or even know why
he has. His completeness needs to be stern, measuring
what he stands to lose. His eyes
are bronze, his heart is bronze with the mystery
of it. Yet it will change his sleep
to have gazed beyond memory, I think, without sadness or
fear onto the flowing backs of horses. I look down
and see that his feet are bare, and I
have never seen such beautiful prideless feet set
on the earth. He must know what he's doing, I think, he
must not need to forgive himself the way I do

because this bounty pours onto me
so I'm crushed by surrender, heaped and

scattered and pounded into the dust with wanting more,
wanting feet like that to drive back
the shame that wants to know why
I have to go through the world like an overwrought
magnet, like the greedy braille of so many
about-to-be-lost memories. Why I can't just
settle down by the side of the road and turn the music
up on one of those raw uncoffined voices of
the dead – Bob Marley, Billie Holiday or the way Piaf
sang "Je Ne Regrette Rien" – so that when

the purled horse in the music asks what I want with it
we are swept aside by there being no answer except
not to be dead to each other, except for
those few moments to belong beyond deserving to
that sumptuousness of presence, so the heart
stays simple like the morality of
a robin, the weight of living so clear a mandate
it includes everything about this junkshop
of a life. And even some of our soon-to-be deadness
catches up to us
as joy, as more horses than we need.

His Shining Helmet; Its Horsehair Crest

I was reading the novel
about a war fought on horseback, reading
with the pleasure of a child given horror as
splendor. The moment came when
the soldier rose in his saddle and
the rim of the saddle was shorn
away. There the story broke off.
Then the survey of fallen comrades and
the field trampled around those with
"wounds to the head and breast." Strange
how I thought of the horses during
these tinted portraits, the horses, mentioned
only as "he rode," "his mount
stumbled," or "he bent from
the saddle to retrieve the standard, then
galloped on."

I close the book and see then
the one they did not speak of – the one
wounded in the face, the one
with his hand caught in the mane of
his horse, which lies beside and
over him, its eyes still open and its breath
a soft plunging to which the novelist
would add a "light rain" or
"a distant thunder of cannons."

But in the closed book, this
is the long moment I look into – the future

in which the wounds, as they say in the manual,
will be "non-specific, though
fatal." How far
from the single admonition in the Hittite cavalry
instructions, simply to: "Kill
the horse."

Refusing Silence

Heartbeat trembling
your kingdom
of leaves
near the ceremony
of water, I never
insisted on you. I admit
I delayed. I was the Empress
of Delay. But it can't be
put off now. On the sacred branch
of my only voice – I insist.
Insist for us all,
which is the job
of the voice, and especially
of the poet. Else
what am I for, what use
am I if I don't
insist?
There are messages to send.
Gatherings and songs.
Because we need
to insist. Else what are we
for? What use
are we?

That Kind of Thing

I'm ready to climb into the shower
at the luxury hotel in Bahia when he
arrives, the Information Officer
from the American Consulate of Salvador.
I'd just said to Ray, "I feel like we've
walked straight into a bank
where they keep people" – and this suite
invented, like the word "posh," by somebody
serious about pleasure in an off-handed
way. And this man – off-
handed too in a khaki shirt so tight on him
the buttons ripple open when he
sits down, revealing little jets of
flesh and chest hair.

So, crossing and uncrossing his
legs, he tells us what to expect: don't
wear jewelry into town or, if we do,
to make sure any chains we wore
were really gold, so when the thieves
yanked them from our necks we
wouldn't be beheaded. A woman had
walked into his office just the other day
with her throat ripped – one of those cheap
metal neck-chains – though he didn't want
to alarm us. And the tourist who met
a man with a pistol outside his hotel who
said to give him his wedding ring and when it
wouldn't come off, the bandit
put the man's finger into his mouth and
sucked on it and said: this ring
is going to come off or I'll bite it

off. Ray lights up a cigarette, maybe even
two cigarettes, and slides the glass
balcony door open so the smoke can go out.
The ocean-sound comes in like an invisible
waterfall standing somewhere in the room
where we sit, eighteen floors up and,
as the receptionist said – not to worry,
"every room with a water view."

"You're just in time to see the sunset,"
says the Information Officer of
Salvador. "But did
the ring come off?" I ask.
"Oh sure," he says, with an air of the less
than trivial, this matter of rings and
fingers. "A lot of poverty here. A lot of
hunger." He's got a year to go in Salvador,
one of those places, he wants us to know, not
on the top of anyone's assignment list, even
a man like him, who's served most of
his time in Third World Countries – the gist
of his feeling being: they don't call them
"under-developed" for nothing.

Discussing then, the plight of
university professors working for so little
they have to hold sometimes three, four jobs –
the Information Officer somehow relating this
to his important friend who
ran a golf course, a food processing plant, and
a restaurant in another town – just to
make ends meet, we supposed, but never made
the connection. "But the students, do they
support the professors in the strike?"
"Oh, sure, students will go with anything

that's against the government. The reactionary
left. They'd like to make a revolution, but
just when they're supposed to
demonstrate – it rains and they cancel
out – or the sun shines and it's such a nice
day they have to go to
the beach. No, it's a hard place
to be a revolutionary," he says, as if he'd
been one himself in some former
incarnation. But he's gone on to more dignified
pursuits as befits a man who represents
a government whose banks have bankrolled debts
so colossal its bankers would have to
confiscate whole countries
to turn this thing around, a man with
diapers to change – with a savvy glance in my
direction, protecting his flank, having dropped
news of his Japanese wife who "poops out"
around 6 p.m. every night. "That woman
loves to cook!" and only the night before
"knocked out a banquet (does all the cooking
herself). May is our busy month." They
haven't seen much of Brazil but got
down to São Paulo where the wife
spotted some hamburger joints and they hit
McDonalds, a Big Boy and a Whopper – one, two,
three – that woman who loves
to cook. Jumping then

to this baby whose diaper might at this very
moment need changing, so he had to
get back, but whatever we needed, not
to hesitate. Give him a call. "That's what
I'm here for," (in this hell hole, he
seemed to want to add). Then as
afterthought, we'd need an interpreter –
"It's a problem. I have to do everything

in Portuguese," he says, as if apologizing for
some deaf mute we'd eventually have to
meet. His hand out to me, but

speaking to Ray: "I read your stuff. Well
written. But, to be perfectly
honest, too depressing. I have to live
with that kind of thing
down here all the time." His hand cast
over his shoulder at the city. "Know
what I mean? But well written." Pumping
my hand then and us
not supposed to hesitate, but the waterfall
drowning out whatever else as the door

closed and we sat back on the couch,
smiling crazily
under the palm fronds
in the smoke-filled vault
with the lights of Salvador
shining in the distance and the Information
Officer of Salvador
gone home to his duties.

Bahia, Brazil. 1984

In Maceio

She gave me the flowers –
two armfuls of red iris backed with
fern fronds and this red, red of
parrot feathers, red
of a death shout, of any heart's
last breath. As we started to move
from the lecture room to leave them
behind, she gave me the flowers.
I said what are they called in
Portuguese? She
smiled, shook her head and no one else
knew either. But she wanted
me to know, she was giving me
the flowers. Not just
decoration on the table behind which
I stood to tell the night students
about poetry in America. They
were dying, these flowers, in the heat of
my English flowing over the tired students.
"But they're stupid, these students,"
Eduardo said. Eduardo who spent his nights
with them and had to
do it, though he meant to love them and
did, working two jobs himself – a professor
on strike at the University, needing more
pay, making it up with these
night students, "these ones" who, he said, wanted
more and who came stupid and mostly stayed
stupid while they got an education.
But she gave me the flowers, picked them up
in her two arms as we started to leave them
behind to be thrown out with

the trash. She gave me
the flowers and I said did you
understand what I said? and she said "Yes,"
maybe the only English she knew and she
put the red flowers with no name
into my arms, and we walked out of there.

Sugar

The restaurant's expensive and German, but
it's Porto Alegre and the American to
my left has just delivered us
like so much pulpy meat
the six hours from Florianopolis, him
driving, he thinks, like a real
Brazilian. But without their confidence in
Death as the one reliable card
in the deck waiting to turn up no matter how
careful you are. So what the hell! Why not
live in the rush of cosmic benevolence tested
by the far side of what limits kill
of desire – instead of letting chance get
flabby, letting your hand
cool on the throttle like a mortician's palm

on your kneecap? But no, this well-meaning
fellow put fear in the car like a huge,
noxious bouquet of forget-me-nots, put
betrayal, put loss in the shape of
his young wife who'd left that very morning
and taken their child with her back to
America and the good life. He flung him-
self at Death like confetti. And I swear
I saw Death dust off his proud shoulders,
shake his black mane, throw back his
huge head and laugh that beautiful
wreck of a laugh that knows
exactly where it's going. Death

doesn't want the bride-
groom. I had opportunity to see that,
between one near-miss and the next

expertly negotiated curve. No, Death is like
a busy man with something else
on his mind while he does
what he's going to
do. The way he took my friend's
husband who'd gone to the garden to dig a few
potatoes for supper. She heard his spade
strike the concrete walkway and saw
through the kitchen window his face pushed
into the soft, dark furrow. So I kept
the conversation live-

ly all the way, while my dear-
est and only slept off terror in the back seat.
Then we arrived at this marvelous feast.
The American to my left, as if
confirming poison in the glass I'd just taken
a drink from, leaned over and said, "Look around
you. You don't see any brown faces here, do
you?" In Rio the brown-faced novelist from
Buenos Aires who said, "They either killed or
deported them. Yes, the faces get whiter
the farther south you go." And yes, the faces

at our table are white, so white
Nora's story about the last time she took sugar
in her coffee stays with me
like a requiem. "We went back to the town
where my mother was raised," she said, watching
the others ladle sugar
into their strong, black coffee. "And there
on the street, we saw
the man who'd been engaged to my mother
at the time my father stole her
away. He was a doctor and everyone in
the family thought he would have made a better

husband than my father. Who knows? Maybe
they were right. We saw him crossing
the street. My father grabbed hold
of my mother like he was afraid she might run
back to him, and said, 'There's that man! Let's

get out of here.' That night when the waiter
offered sugar, my father said, as he always said,
'No sugar.' I must have been feeling some
solidarity with my father because when the waiter
came to me, I also said, 'No sugar.' I was
thirteen years at the time and it
was the 6th of February, 1947. From that day on
I have never taken sugar in
my coffee – a real Oedipus
complex." Then someone in the company corrected
her and said, "No, a real *Electra*
complex." And everyone agreed and said the word
Electra, either outloud or
to themselves, *Electra,* as they tasted for a
moment, the sugar – the sweet black
sugar in those thick cups of coffee we were about
to drink together.

If Blood Were Not as Powerful as It Is

From the open market with its tangy smell
of salted meats and caged birds into
this coolness – the Golden Chapel
of Recife where Christ too is gold-
encrusted and the rays spiking
from his golden head
set off the irregular rays of blood
streaming down his forehead, blood which
would be golden too, if blood
were not as powerful as it is – powerful
enough to avoid even gold.

We sign the guest book and stand
before the glass showcase
where another Christ, lit up like
an expensive jewel, reclines
with his knees slightly
bent. A rivulet trickles from his rib cage
and stops without dropping
one precious drop – this heavenly body
that bleeds without bleeding.

In a dark alcove, a third Christ
is displayed on his back.
I can't see his face. Monks beckon
to either side and I see he is dressed
as they are, in the brown robe
of the Third Order of St. Francis.
The soles of his long, thin feet, each
with the blood-sign where the missing nails
joined him to the cross, are tilted
into view where he lies on the wooden cart.

Then I notice Mary – the black arches
of her eyebrows lifted so they mean she
will plead for eternity and not be
answered as she gazes upon these replicas
of what was her son – his own eyes
peacefully closed in a beauteous pain
that flows outward the more he tries
to hold it in. And she,
the woman in the doorway as we start to leave,

has asked for and is given
a glass into which the attendant is pouring
water from a bottle kept
for that purpose. Someone
hovers behind her and she brushes them away
as she drinks, so as to drink
deeply enough to get past the fear of the next
thirsting. She drinks
and lifts her eyes, drinks and
watches, then calls

to the other and offers up the glass to be
filled again, which the attendant does,
obedient, for now, to what our guide calls
"the informal sector." Then I remember
at the Consulate, talk of drought
five years running in regions
to the South, how these people have come
into the cities for food, for
water. The face
behind her shoulder looks up: Mary
of Recife, who needs water, who
lets him give her
the water
she has been waiting for.

Recife, Brazil. June, 1984

Redwing

The readers of poetry, the writers of
poetry. Nation inside
the nation. That rainbow holding briefly over
the Strait of Juan de Fuca, its violet
inner rim, its guess-work dome
of crimson. My back to the sun for this
to happen at all, the eye extending
its shadow until it sees into
what it doesn't see. I don't have to think
of raindrops hanging as light, or to command
the schoolbook corpses of refraction and
internal reflection to be dazzled. The myth
of the Vilela Indians, its rainbow
a gigantic serpent charmed
by a small girl until it sheds her
sway and piecemeal ravages the world, vanquished
at last by an army of birds – that's good enough
for me. And victory too, each bird
dipping itself in the blood
of the monster.

With Stars

for M. K.

My mother speaks from the dark – why
haven't I closed my eyes? Why don't I
sleep? And when I say I can't, she
wraps the quilt around me and leads me
to the window. I am four years old and
a star has the power of wishes.
We stare out together, but she sees past
their fierce shimmering sameness, each
point of light the emblem
of some lost, remembered face. What
do they want? I ask. "Not to be
forgotten," she says, and draws me close.
Then her gaze sifts the scattered brilliance.
Her hand goes out – "There! that one!" so
her own mother, dead years back, looks down
on us. Sleep then like a hammer
among the orbiting dead.

Tonight it is the stars reminding
keeps me up past midnight.
My mother's voice, as in that childhood room,
is with me so surely I might rush out
and find that window, those stars
no further than the next doorway, and her
there waiting – awake all night
because I was awake. "Go
to sleep," I'd say. "They want me
awake tonight." And she'd know who I meant –

those others still living and afar
because I think them there. And why not
give the dead this benefit of separations?
There were so many nameless before.
But oh, if one falls, *if* –
how can that child ever fall asleep
until sunrise?

Dim House, Bright Face

She still cries over that dead child,
and for years would bring him up
with strangers who came to the house.
Unashamed to weep freshly, she took again
the cheaply framed school photograph
and passed it from hand to
hand. The boy's open gaze into that forward time,
laden then with calamity
because it seemed, to the minds of those unwary
visitors, that he knew his silence
had another meaning, one that entered
theirs and caused those moments to almost
make a sound they each
withheld.

So she softened his ongoing future in her heart
with their unreceivable comfort. Took
back the photograph and put it
in the drawer, as if to shield him
from their inrushing eagerness
to hear of those other faces on the mantle,
the ones who can't know yet what living
was.

The Borrowed Ones

for Caroline Bock

We, the old children, are now old again
with a new authority. We take
their young hands in ours
and tell them we will stay old, swear
to grow even older, be rust
to their iron. Whose are these
rain barrels in the pasture that fill and over-
fill with softest rain? I knock them aside
and the ground drinks, in its gradual way,
all they give.

We were the motherless, or those who say "Mother"
as "help me," and whatever comes – that sky
with one orange bird, even a wave
that endures moonlight – even these
will do. Finally we did
for ourselves. In our loving we mothered
the men we wanted to be more than. And
though our breasts were still the breasts of
children, we gave ourselves as children
give, with the door wide open, with
the house on fire. Still, our hands were
mothers' hands, were lament and pledge,
a whirl of bells through the sweet gloom of
their foraging, and, yes, something, something was
satisfied.

If at our table those who would have loved us
ate the meal, forgetting to light
the candles, we smiled on them
with the kindness of conquered stars – not
the brightest ones, but those

expendable ones
that fall to gain a share
in the splendor.

Now, if I call you "Daughter," it is not
out of obedience
you will step toward me
but as the ghost of one who bore you,
gazing out – I, who have given you
a daughter's arms.

All Day the Light Is Clear

Today I wished without mercy
in the bloodless nations of the mind
that a city had gone down with you
as in a war fought – not
on foreign soil, but here
in the part of the country I can't
do without. Then, if I wept for you
inexplicably, as I have
on street corners, I could say the name
of that city and ignite in the memories
of strangers, a companion
sorrow. "Yes," they would say, "Yes,
we know," giving again that name
like a fountain
in some dusty village where the women pause,
dash water across their brows,
and pass on.

And though I shame such power and force it
from my mind, you enter this street
as a touch on the shoulder, a stare that
speaks, or in the brief nods
between workers at change of shift.
I lean on their conquering faces.
I add you to the heap, to the beautiful
multitude for whom only singing
and silence may serve – those
of our city, city of the unmiraculous,
undiminished belonging, toward which
in the green fields – as did the women
of Leningrad – I bow, bow again
and make no sound.

Their Heads Bent
Toward Each Other Like Flowers

Those who hold themselves above suicide,
(and who could blame them?) would
make a joke of your efforts and how we both
survived. Sometimes I can't help myself and
a shred of the story slips out of the silence –
how I came into that house we shared
near the wise, gray Atlantic and, as one bewildered,
you showed me where the pistol went off suddenly,
unexpectedly, before you could lift it
to your head. "There," you said, and we looked up
to the neat bird-sized entry
in the plaster, stood like two guilty children
who've struck all the matches
in the empty house and singed away
their delicate eyebrows.

Again we stand – young husband, uncertain wife –
as I tell this to someone for whom it cannot matter,
though this too is necessary – to feel such minds
turn away, as mine did then
in worse than disbelief.
I was too safe in my young woman's body, too precious
as one is precious before the imagined death
one intends to accomplish later, much
later, and, if possible, only in poems
where the choosing is huge, is classic and belongs
to time, as we do not who serve no future. Or so
you tried, in your failed way, to tell me – I

who could not be loved, and so
seemed eternal.

Yours was that other bravery, the one worth mocking.
You lived on past your chosen death, and I,
who had a life, this ring of smoke
these fifteen years, at last emerge into another,
premature vacancy, bounded on all sides
with beginnings – this altered memory in which
the shot, as you intended, passes through us both,
and we are not here to end the story
with love and live on as we must.

Or perhaps love is only the apology
I invent to hold your place – until even that claim
is not needed, and you reappear
as one stronger even than memory, ungarlanded
by its sullen excess, its shadow-music
thrummed against the skull. At this threshold
you are willing even to do without
love – as I cannot – willing
at last to be forgotten.

Photograph of a Lighthouse Through Fog

I said: dark voyage, I am deeply wounded
    and desire still in me
        like an eel.
I said: shards and trembling.
Said: the golden light of the sea.
Said: I can not separate your light from
        your silence.

This reaches him like a photograph
of the lighthouse on a clear day. What is it
    for? this disabled
        windmill, this moon
    in armor?

    The rest without cunning or blame.
    Fog
rolls in with its 'vale of the soul,' its
    fledgling obedience, daring to ask:
        where are we now?
        Caught in some ruby-throated
pain; its staple of hope
        mercenary as the word
    eternity.

I said: vigil and a body that dies.
I said: heart not of this shore, the birds fly
        through me.
Said: I once lived dark
    like honey, deepest in
        pleasure after the pleasure.
Said: halo, memory dampens my
    memory. I can't know

how far I shine.

Pain, he said, is advice I never take. Any cat
knows what to do in the aviary.

The photographer lashes the camera to his arm,
              hoping to record light as
                   inscription, its
                              baptismal slapping
              against the water.
                   But is
that salty staccato warning or invitation?

              Stay away, I said. *Stay
                        away.*

Small Garden Near a Field

While any two are talking, one,
without glimpsing it, has already shed
the confident smile of the living. You
were going first all our childhood. Youngest
of my brothers, I used you up, squandered
your fifteen years which can't remember itself
in its voiceless purpose. "Twenty-three-years
today he's gone," our mother said, as you ran
to the dresser to bring my hair brush. Twenty-
three-years as you put on your many coats, as you
bicycled through the neighborhood slinging newspapers
like fury onto porches in the crisp half-dawn.

How dead you wanted to be when you died! Each
stuttering moment pearled in the memory – how
I let you lean out of the dark into my car window
the night of your first prom. I can smell
the brash carnation in your buttonhole, imagine
the youngest kisses, those given innocently
before desire rakes like a searchlight across
the cool, the cruel valleys of love you
will never have. You click shut, kiss
shut, and won't live to April.

I roll down the window. You rest
your arms on my arm, grin shyness over
the chipped front tooth and don't want to say much
in front of her, the girl in taffeta and longing –
your first, last girl. Get in, I say, let's
cruise by where we don't live anymore. That house
a shack now, brambles and kids' toys, the willow
sagging into the street. It's right

to drive by, harm ourselves a little with
what comes after, push back
the goodness of the past so it doesn't cry out

unattainable. Goodness of
not enough beds so they sent you
into mine to be thralled sleepward with stories.
Language to you is still errand and magic
spiced with singing. I close my eyes
and remember yours open. I'm already a reader
of books, have begun to work that slow trench into
history. Babur – I tell you like treasure –
was the first Mughal Emperor of India, descended
from Ghengis Khan and Timur
the Lame. Babur: Turkish for lion.

They have wrapped your head in gauze, my sultan,
the folds of your turban make a temple
where you lie. The conquering is over now
and we are laying out the garden you planned,
patterned after the remembered one
in Kabul. It won't be enough. "In Agru," you say,
"they have no horses, no grapes or muskmelon, no
ice or cold water, no baths or candles, no torches,
not a candlestick." I snail your warmth
into mine, sleep night-long, death-long beside you,
legend to your unlived name which I carry
like a dead tree
with the live birds still in it.

Present

She could hold me with stories, even
those about people whose names and doings
were feathers, a fluttering at
the brain, scattered or wafted in the current
of her voice, softly away. Those lives
happened out of her and into me and out
again, because I couldn't remember, only be
warmed by them. Somehow my forgetting insured
returns to that hovering population in her
memory, of which, as I found, I was a part.

She said she thought maybe she couldn't have
children, maybe nothing would come. She
and my father together by then two years.
His being dead now, not coming into this, but
there too, as if he couldn't hear us,
but we could know for him. "I'd go up into
the woods where he was logging, do what I could,
work hard as two men myself. That day

on Round Mountain your dad and his partner
got ahead of me. I'd been working.
I hadn't seen where I was. Suddenly I was
alone, walking this old logging road, fireweed
over my head. I stood still and listened
to the birds and other sounds – wind and
little fallings and shiftings in the undergrowth,
animal stirrings. It's so beautiful
here! I kept thinking. I've never been anywhere
so beautiful! I was alone with the mountain. Sun

shattering down through the trees onto ferns
and fallen logs. It's peaceful here, I thought.
Then it came to me, like the mountain had told
me, and I knew it was over. One waiting was
over. And another was starting. The feeling so
sure I put my hands on my belly and pressed
a little against where the carrying had started
before I'd known it. Knowing then, so you'd
stopped happening without me. "We," I thought,
"*We.*" And I thought of your father not

knowing yet, and it seemed you were knowing for
him already, were rushing ahead of me like
an action I had no part in, but was all of me
and some of him that I was about to let you tell
him. Isn't that what conception is? Agreeing
to take the consequences of things so far
beyond you that a trembling takes over and more
is shaken out of us than we can
possibly account for?" And something else, she
said, the elevation of mountains, the way

beauty makes things want to join
each other. Then far off, like an echo of
itself, the *swish-swish* of the crosscut,
the steady rhythm of the blade limber against
a tree. She started to walk, still thinking how
beautiful it was all around her, the partnership
of the saw blade raking through the silence
as she made her way toward the far away
splintering, the rending of the heartwood she
knew would fall, would crash down, shuddering

the length of itself against the trees still
standing, while like a deer, picking its way
through underbrush to the edge of
the clearing, she moved, until
they saw her back into human shape. A woman
whose whereabouts they had wondered vaguely
about as they worked. And as she joined them,
they kept on with their working.

Cougar Meat

Carried this morning in the dodge and swoop
of error, rethinking a breach
with a friend – how I'd failed to staunch harm
with kindness when she needed me
as sacrifice – then you, brother, came in
to say goodbye, hovered in my kitchen
for coffee. You'd been hunting cougar three days
and nights, with your dogs, somewhere
in the mountains back of Gardiner. You hadn't
slept, keeping the fever up until the magic
gave in to you. But on the third day
snow, the invisible current of pursuit
exchanged for tracks. The kill then, baffling
and simple – awesome death made perfunctory
with a shot. I hear you out, know why

you've come, certain of welcome, yet your act
hated for the usual "female" reasons, or so
you think, and are freed of wonder and of
shame. Should I ask, Pharaoh, did you eat
of the heart? Did you find it sweet? Or,
in a bounty of silence, know the pelt
torn away, the carcass unquenchable where it fell
in its blue efficiency, its avalanche of
unmeaning which allows those man-sized footsteps
to point away unknown, yet deeply familiar. Mine
to ask whose wildness we are, whose trust
soon to be plundered? The adrenalin has let you
down. You're bone-weary and back with
the rest of us, diamond bright with hunger,

unfulfilled by the dominant courage here toward
livelihood with all its unedifying hazards.
Should I put aside kinship with the hunted and
the dumb, pray that cougars last for men like you?
Only in the mind's rarefied traffic with the sacred
have I met cougar. Could have gone all day, all
life not thinking *cougar,* had you kept
from here. Wild Horse Annie, in that same untutored
leap, defended mustangs in the Pryor Mountains,
never having laid eyes on one. Enough to guess
spirits of the West surviving in those rugged bands
pursued by helicopters. Her fear – the unseen loss,
more heritage in a Medicine Hat Pinto than
in the frontier mandate to take what

you can. "Good eating too," you say, still
talking cougar. "The word is, it tastes like pork
or veal, not that I'd know." You launch into story:
"That time Dad forgot his lunch and one of the guys
on the dock offered him a sandwich, which he
ate. At poker break, he said to the guy, 'What
kind of sandwich was that, anyway?'
'Me-ow!' the guy said, and he didn't mean pussycat.
Dad looked at him, said 'It's better than snake,
by God, better than flying squirrel, and I've
eat both with appetite to spare.' Cougar meat!" my
brother says, like somebody has handed him a bat
on a skewer. *Not nature, but the visions she*

gave me, Rilke said. I kiss your cheek, brother,
where we stand on the porch. You're off
on your first vacation to an exotic place – Hawaii,
paradise regained, where you will lie down with
the lamb. You tell me you want your son brought up
to hunt cougar. If you die tomorrow in a plane crash,

I'm supposed to see to that. Don't
count on it, I say. Not one iota have I moved you,
but all day I wear dread in your name, and in the name
of Cougar, renewing in heart the biblical sacrifice of
Uzzah, whose unthinking touch on the Ark of the Covenant
was death to him, instruction for us. Recovering
that clear shot in the snow, these intricacies
of undoing, for which language was also given
to say: the meat was not wasted.

Message for the Sinecurist

The poet of nouns has left my attic.
Burn the wood, I said. Read
my books. Sleep under my roof, dream
and prosper. One thing in recompense
I asked. So was he late or
never, and made a landlord
of a friend. So was he my tenant
and missed the premise of those rooms
and rooftops.

When we had cleared away his locus
of debris, we sat and read his postcard
from the beauteous far place – clearly
his intentions so full of spine
and keen regret, but haste and sadness
had paraphrased him badly. We considered,
then put the card away.

I sit under the high pitch of rain again
and the birds thread through my days
with fresh regard. Yes, nouns, the nails,
the vigorous scaffold of each elected tree.
But then, my poet, the awful hammering
that knows as it does.

Simple Sonatina

Something is dying, but without blood or
writing on any shore. Everything seems as
it was: no poets dignified with prison, none
banished or tortured. Each of us
has enough paper to write the histories of
several worlds. We don't fear the knock
at the door. And yet, this stench, this
oversweet stillness reaches even here
among the nations of spruce and hemlock,
head-high salal and the thorny devil's club.
That country I could speak with intimately
in myself, country Whitman honored, teeming
and lustrous, country I crossed and recrossed
like a thrown-out child until anywhere
wasn't home – something of that country

has made its dying spot in the woods,
and, slug-bellied with salvage, crawls away.
These are lying times, my friends, lying times.
Easy to say the varnished brutes want to cozy up
again, when *again* convicts. No heroics here.
I don't regret a single poem about "the tawny-
throated nightingale," or simple duty
which "hath no place for fear," or Longfellow's
"soft bells, and gleaming nights." But something
of what I loved is alone in me now, as it is
for many who loved so. In this indifferent time
harmony wears too amiable a face, and I can't sing
"Melancholy Baby" any more.

The Story of a Citizen

Rain extravagantly that morning kept us
at the coffee shop, discussing what? Our era?
Not too grand to say – yes, and with the fervor
of young philosophy students. *Our* era which,
Alan said, would be known for its blatant political
pornography: "No contours, only oscillating
transitions," a phrase he applied like a seasoning
of butterflies to astound us past meaning. "It
makes me want to puke," Jerry said every so often.
"What does?" somebody finally asked. "All of it,"
he said. Outside the rain coming down, insisting
on reverie, no one able to summarize the gut feeling
of having been stripped of the sacred on more than
one front, though it came down to that. Just
listening made you hunger for extremities,

anything to get beyond the synthetic equilibrium
of helplessness. Why not attempt the truly brazen?
Your friend's elevation of a dead dog into
negotiable value – this impressed you. You read
his novel twice, thinking he'd found the key
to selflessness. Yet dogs seemed so obvious, so
eminently popular. Kick one and a regiment of
defenders will taint your history. But,
like a government casting about for the right
passion to assist its military decor, a kick
was needed: so you kicked. Call it an evil instinct,
but there I was, as we scurried back to our jobs
in the downpour, a woman stopping to kick a dog that
had been tied to a parking meter, which already
insinuated that the dog wished to be elsewhere. My
kick had the authority of ownership, so no one passing

bothered to confuse it with cruelty, or fun.
The primitive takes over and raises such events beyond
interpretation into what might be called a "detached
commission." My kick was a serious kick, not based
on chance or deserving, but on the priorities of
ownership – which is an American pastime – to empty
that office of pleasure, to subdue it to the purely
civilian. I am thinking here of a ballet dancer who
praised the essentially military "when put to civilian
uses," who said: "I enjoyed the Army very much indeed.
I was a courier. I was an interpreter. . . . I had my own
jeep." As the courier of my kick I acknowledged
the tyranny of being addressed as a civilian while
the oneiric appearance of weapons loomed symphonic
with extinction in the vestibule. This then becomes

the history of how I became a soldier – I,
whose only patriotic act had been the continued
love of myself in the body of a woman.
A woman forced through soldierly fear to
rejuvenate a childhood relationship with God.
A woman twice visited by ownership in marriage,
who invested tumultuously in the promise of love
eternal because it appealed to her among the other
friendly disengagements. That woman, that
self-appointed kicker of dogs, conscripted now
like every other woman, man and dog: woman who
waits uneasily for orders, who despises
her superiors, who once was a mist of tenderness,
who exudes savagery, who is apolitical which is
the tribe of the soldier, who sleeps like a corpse
at the feet of her master, who squirms

in the ranks, who thinks, "A short nap
in the snow would be exceedingly nice," whose
memory of a home-cooked meal has been obliterated
by the seepage of fear, whose hair was first cut
at the age of thirteen, whose flower is
the butterfly bush, who will die a civilian
among other civilian-cum-soldiers, whose enemy
is an evil instinct with an expanding agenda,
whose campaign is the Campaign Under Moonlight
which requires that she bay like a wolf
speaking through moonlight which is the hotline
to the spirits of her ancestors, telling them
of their civilian descendants, of dogs
and the masters of dogs, through which she was

domesticated, this wolf, who honors itself
as a woman, who carries the dead
in her body, whose name is Spako, meaning
"Bitch," for she does as she pleases, whose
curses have the power to come true, who can see
ghosts, whose star is the brightest, is
the Eye of the Dog, whose threshold is guarded
by the poets because they know the sacredness
of doorways, of ancient cornerstones, under which
are the sacrificed, the bodies of the saints,
the civilian saints, to whom I swear allegiance,
though saint is a word in poverty
when the memories of nations die with them,
as our time would require of us: as the folk dance
begins, as we scorn such death.

Survival of a Heart

So few particles of bodyhood engine
their way past oblivion, that when it keeps
being the heart that's saved I have to
listen, consort with mine in its pleasant lair,
assume its rustling more dearly. Though why not
cherish the bladder or the nose, those in and
outs immune to honeycombs of soul
devices? Why not one poet to exalt "Oh melancholy
elbow, oh chin, oh sweet pituitary, oh matchless
epiglottis!" To have been erotogenically sealed
by flat earth poesy makes me haunt
in my prime. Give me the mound and scoop
of fortune, Keats lingering on "a naked waist," or
Dickinson with moss on her lips, before I
dive this interior earthward. If after all
the Egyptians prevail and heart is
the requisite miser fit only to fling back at
gods who fondle and foul us, you, little dancer,
must tell it all – what scrapes and scraps and
summer lightning we had in the body's
swallow. Meanwhile, think on Voltaire's demise:
last minute maneuvers with the clergy to avert
the lime pit, then parcelled out, his brain to
the apothecary, his heart secured by
the Marquis de Villette, his body
driven off in one coach, his heart in
another, the coffin retrieved after thirteen years
from Scellières, "brought in triumph" to Paris,
installed in the Panthéon, the coffin opened
finally to pay homage but found empty having been

pillaged by fanatics, its contents thrown
onto the rubbish heap. The jar wherein sloshed
his brain sold at auction to an unknown
buyer, the heart – that long suffering scoffer –
bequeathed to the Bishop of Orléans who put it
on the block. Napoleon III "acquired" it, gave it
to the National Library in Paris where, as
the biographer said, it sits "next to the products
of his brain." Now, little coach, go your way.

Into the Known

for Bill Knott

A corpse has walked across my shadow.
How do I know? I was standing
so it fell darkly across the shadow of a tree
in water, and my shadow grabbed hold
in the branches and shouted, "I'm drowning!
Save me!" Okay, I said, and stepped
to the side a few paces, disengaging its
arms from the leaves rippling through
me. But two boys rowed over it, dipping
their oars through my breasts and
groin. "Save yourself!" my shadow cried.
But when I walked jauntily upstream, it
scraped along behind as usual, sure of
itself as a corpse is sure, so it speaks
to no one, yet holds our attention resentfully
like a cow in the roadway.

A gull rowed over me and I felt
feverish, as if my future meant to initiate
a moment I would soon have to avoid.
Time to rehabilitate your astonishment, I said
to myself and plunged on
into the known. A carriage
with two cream-colored horses pulls up, as I
knew it would, and my shadow gets out. She
comes up to me like she means to slap me,
but I turn my back quick! so she falls
over the necks of the horses and they tremble
and jangle their bits and lift their hooves
smartly in place on the pavement.

Yes, today a corpse put its inaugural hand
on my shoulder, on my shadow's silken
shoulder, like a sword through meringue.
Veil of white, veil of drowned breath – I was
sticky with it, plundered like a wren's nest.
Down I lay in the grass and down
like a dog to roll, but my shadow jumped
into me – retouching the real with
the real, as the mortician said.
Pianissimo, dread fumbled the length of me,
a safari of butterflies skimming the lunge
of a gravesite. I kept breathing

as long as I could, convulsively snatching
the breaths back into me, but my mind
kept seeing a sailboat with its sail
gone slack. And because I know something about
wind, how it fidgets and stampedes, then
forgets entirely so everything goes still,
I folded my hands on my breasts
and let things take their course, and let
the sun shine deeply upon me, and let
the carriage sulk near the walnut grove,
and the cream-colored horses neigh to other
horses and, in starlight, cloud-shadows
drowsy as a mind that can't shout, can't
beseech – let these drift over the beloved
corpse of my shadow. Suddenly then

I pull myself up! "Not me!" I say.
I make them dance – that mitten, my shadow –
that quisling, my corpse. I dance
like a woman led to a vault of spiders.
I tell the horses to
dance too. I still don't know
if we got out of it.

The Hands of the Blindman

In the square room
without windows
where the hours fill our pockets
with soft money, you reach
for simple things: the circle
of ash, the cup, its warm
liquid eye, the telephone, its knowing
that voices are always blind.

Walking from work, you wave fire
past your cigarette. There
is the hand of the stranger, now
the muzzles of dogs, the
rain. Touching my face once, you
were the rain, the stranger –
yet never did anyone in the dark
leave hands on me as you.

Rijl

To be a child named after a star
is to be given earth and heaven too, never
to find the dark unpossessive where you stand,
enraptured to the ground. Foot
of the Giant, Rijl al Musalsalah – Foot of the Woman
in Arabic, Heaven's Great General to
the Chinese who invented lotus feet for their women –
not just the foot miniaturized, but folded so
the underside of heel and
toes press together to blunt each step with
helplessness. Such a walker

I saw once near the Forbidden Palace
in Beijing, accompanied by her granddaughter.
Their hobbled steps still fresh to the mind that knows
there were poets who praised this exchange of pain
for beauty. I stumble among these duller earth-stars
to hang giants of another kind, so that from your sky
overflowing with immortals, you will look down
as we look up, to feel distance as kinship, splendor
as the white heads of our mothers. Algebar,
who must step as the giant bids, even

into the sea, though empowered
to survive there. Read in the legend
his interlude of blindness, how he wept on the shore –
Orion-the-hunter, the cannibal god-giant of Egypt
inscribed on the tombs as Sahu, a man running
with his head turned over his shoulder, "fleet
of foot, wide of step." And what is blindness but
the head upended in the foot so the body is all temple
or none? Intention, that willful god
of the strong, can't send a swallow from clocktower to

clothesline, yet you, child, sweep up the room, and
dancing with your arms over your head, command
to be joined, for yours is a double star, white-hot
and tinged with blue. I am your giant,
delivered to sight, going heart-in-heart
where you lead. Rai al Jauzah, herdsman of the stars,
it is winter where I write, and you are gleaming
above the hemlock, talisman
of a guardian joy. Not to you, but to the real girl
I turn, recalling a night when, dashing
from the house, she refused her sweater, calling back
for us all, "Don't you know I'm
a star? Don't you know
                    I'm burning up?"

Bonfire

for Ray

The inflections of joy. The inflections of
                    suffering. And strangely
            sometimes the mixing
                    of the two.
It reminds me of opening the huge *International*
            Butterfly Book with over 2000 species
                    illustrated in color
            and among them, the giant birdwing butterfly
                    Ornithoptera victoriae
obtained when John McGillivray, aboard the *HMS*
                            Rattlesnake
            used a shotgun to bring it down
                    somewhere in the Pacific.
Other wild petals shattered by use of
                    pronged arrows
                            in New Guinea.
And the laughable "mechanical butterfly" intended
            as a decoy, said to be "very successful" in
                    capturing the flashing
                            blue Morpho.

So many kinds of crying. So much raw gaiety,
            variegated with glittering
                    silence. And you,
            my sudden bouquet,
who came to me awkwardly at the head of the stairwell
            outside the room that sheltered
                    for so many nights
            our sleeping and loving.
                    To weep there
                            together

with my death all handsomely in view,
                              all open before us
              as the sea at night.
                  All tenderly
              wild in that calm.

Safe midnight, your arms strong to hold my face into
                              yours
              while the miracle of living raked
              its silky rapier down our backs.
The last time I kissed a man in fear
                  my first love went to war.
But I kissed you anyway – that seal of life, letter
                      sent and received
                                  in an instant.

Once in Quebec I drank cognac in the snow and
                                  on a dare
              ice skated with my
                  friend's violin.
I'd been falling all day, diving into flesh
                      like a spirit half
                  in, half out
                      of the world.
But give me a perishable, fragile beauty
              that belongs to someone else and I skate
                  like music, like
                      the wizard of
                          the hopeful.
How many times I saved myself on behalf of
              that borrowed, that shuddering
                          violin!
When I handed it back he played his bonfire
                      of thanksgiving. Played
              a mazurka, then a jig, then

something vast
and aching
as when love must go on and at the same time
perish.

I'm talking about memory now, that moment
in which the doctor's news
flushed us through with dread,
and I hadn't swerved
back yet
into life. Even then I didn't forget you, violin
who threw yourself into my arms,
violin asking not to
be broken one more time.
It wasn't for music
you came to me, but
for daring – mine
and yours.
When they have to, they will write in the Book
of Welcome:

Two darings, two darlings.

Amplitude

Twice this Christmas Day you tried
to get somebody to listen with
you to the new Ricky Scaggs tape somebody
gave you, and were
refused. You bummed cigarettes, ate
some hot pickles, ranged in and
out of the house, played a game of
"Fish" with your kids, dangling
a magnet from a string
over eight little magnet-mouthed
fish that snapped open their yaps, then
clamped shut before your mag-
net could suck onto them and lift
them out of the wind-up pond
on the coffee table. Your kids beat
you and laughed about
it. You laughed
too, a little. Then clearly
had to find something else
to do. Dinner settled in on our mother, her
mouth open to that other magnet, sleep,
drawing her god knows where
out of our warm, swirling pond of family and
the still excited clutter of gift-
giving. Then you remembered Ray's Mercedes

parked near the swing set and said to me, "Let's
go, Sis," handing me the Scaggs tape. Imposs-
ible, though, to get out of
the house without your wife, Jean, and the
kids who wanted not
to miss out. Errands thought of too, so
it wouldn't be *just*

a ride, presents could be dropped
off to friends so there'd be some place to go
to. All of this okay. And the company
of your kids and wife adding
to the solitude
because of how they travel like a beautiful wake
behind you even when you're alone and
silent at your work. So the car

gliding effortlessly through the nearly
vacant streets, under the sparse dec-
orations of this mill town where we
were born, were kids together. Now, buckled in
to the dark, we adjust the volume and let
the cowboy sing his way down mainstreet, a
place he'll never see, with strangers he could care
less about. "Will you shut up so I can hear
the song, for Chrissake," you say into the back
seat, and, for a while we are all
with you, listening, because you said to, me
waiting until enough listening has gone by
to chance singing along, as you know
I have to, but not minding because it
beefs up the harmonies, a live track angling
in on studio vigor with the discrepancies
of the human. Real enjoyment leading then to

past hardship, so memory, that other fresh-
ness, cuts in to add value in a parallel key: "Did
you ever think, when we were kids and bare-
foot in the logging camps, we'd drive up Race
Street in a Mercedes listening to cowboy
music?" We blotted out a bar
or two of aggressive banjo just marveling
at the unlikelihood. Vaguely, the
sense we shouldn't take such uncomplicated pleasure in

for long, or a magnet might
drop straight through the
roof and snatch one of us a-
way. Then, one by one,
the rest. But delight, pure and
simple, thanks to Ray's Mercedes, for having
pulled a fast one on this town and the in-
visible net over all, that said: You
won't amount to
a damn. And the triumph of it not even ours

as we passed the cemetery, lightly
dusted with snow, and our father there
with the others who came to this place and called
it good enough to hold a life and let it
go – some even, like him, who intended
to die here. The importance
of that choice unmade for me and humming along
with us. Then, looking over at you still
listening to the music, not
singing, but thinking about death or
whether or not you should be ashamed to be
seen motoring through the streets of our
hometown in the guise of those we'd learned to
hate as having more than their share. What

happened to those rocks we rushed from the house
to fling at bumper-to-bumper Californians, dragging
their mobile homes and over-
sized boats past the shack we were raised
in? In what far country did they
land, those heart-flung shards
of our untutored contempt? Here. They
landed here. And pelt down on me
because the violence of a kid's arm
is attached to more than stones and what

the world thinks of anyone's chances. Who's
to say if we could swing down Caroline Street and
pick up those two vigilantes they wouldn't
climb in – glad to have such mild
benefactors – ride along in wordless
awe, then the minute we put them out, set to
with a slingshot? Meanwhile I'm bartering
in the black markets of the mind for

the peace of a front yard nativity where
a kid's bike has tipped refreshingly onto the
baby Jesus so the spokes enhance his re-
solve toward bliss. Belief – the unspectacular
locomotion of childhood, gleams unremittingly
at me through the backlit curtains of
the house – that pyramid of wooly
lights anchored in the shadowy boughs. All
silent. All calm. House after
house. Until we hit
town and a little life stirs
outside the M & C tavern, two women
piloting a wobbly man into a back seat, then
genial shadows as they too climb in, reach
for the ignition and jerk away
from the curb. Suddenly over us a sign

above the used car lot: "Save Ethiopia! Send
money now." Our town shoots out into the starlit
map of the world where last night's TV news-
caster, in a voice dulled by the
ritualization of caring, hovers in-
visibly over a mother who has crawled forty miles
through desert with her child tied to
her back and will, he gives us
to understand, likely die
anyway. The bounce in the ad-break following

hurtles resourcefully on: "In a moment, how *you*
can pick up the tab on African hunger."
Ricky Scaggs careens into another verse
of relentless heartbreak, but it can't lift
an eyelid to this. Nor, inexplicably, that day

my high school chum, driving me down
Blue Mountain Road in his first car, hit
a child's puppy that had run in front of the
car, killing it outright. The kid weeping and
cuddling the mess and my friend, in a frenzy
of remorse, fumbling a dollar bill into
the kid's shirt pocket, then wordlessly sliding
into the seat beside me to drive us
away. That action waving now like a white flag
of surrender over a trench whose once embattled
defenders are safely imprisoned
elsewhere. Passing now the pulp mill and

my brother reminding me how our father
worked there three times, and quit
three times. The windows are fogged
with dirt and ingots of unhealthy,
fluorescent unlight. "Imagine
day after day working in there," I say, thankful
to dispose of a safely impossible fate
so near at hand. My brother looks hard at
the place, then like he could bash it
to bits, his voice low and even: "Jean's dad
spent thirty-nine years
in there." She makes a sharp
noise in the dark to let her father out
again and into his well-earned death. We drive

onto the spit of land that lets us look back
across the harbor at the lights of

the town. More red
in their glimmer tonight, I think, and then,
more gold. "It's
pretty," Jean says, "isn't
it?" The kids in their surplus of quiet, dreamily
then, "Yes, pretty. Really
pretty." We idle in the excellent rigor of
engine-pull de-
signed by Germans, until the same
child-voices, discarding beauty and
death as unequal to the moment, plead us
back "in time," as they put it, to give – unopened,
the gifts we are bearing.

The jacket art is "Laguna Azul" by Alfredo Arreguín.
(Collection of Bellevue Art Museum)

This book was designed by Tree Swenson.

The Galliard type used in this volume was
composed by Fjord Press Typography.

Other Poetry From Graywolf